Education for Leadership
and Social Responsibility

DATE DUE

To Steve Blader

Education for Leadership and Social Responsibility

Gloria Nemerowicz and Eugene Rosi

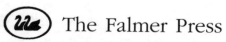 The Falmer Press

(A member of the Taylor & Francis Group)
London • Washington, D.C.

quare, London, EC4A 3DE
s Inc., 1900 Frost Road, Suite 101,

© G. Nemerowicz and E. Rosi 1997

First published in 1997

A catalogue record for this book is available from the British Library

Library of Congress Cataloging-in-Publication Data are available on request

ISBN 0 7507 0608 2 paper

Jacket design by Caroline Archer

Typeset in 11/13pt Garamond by
Graphicraft Typesetters Ltd., Hong Kong.

Printed in Great Britain by Biddles Ltd., Guildford and King's Lynn on paper which has a specified pH value on final paper manufacture of not less than 7.5 and is therefore 'acid free'.

Every effort has been made to contact copyright holders for their permission to reprint material in this book. The publishers would be grateful to hear from any copyright holder who is not here acknowledged and will undertake to rectify any errors or omissions in future editions of this book.

Contents

v

List of Tables and Figures

List of Tables and Figures

Preface

Some authors report that after an initial inspiration, the 'book wrote itself'. That has not been our experience. In fact, we lived this book long before we wrote it. As academic administrators, with our identities still firmly in faculty roles, it didn't take long before the question of 'larger purpose' intruded itself into the administrative routine. In most institutions, there is little time, and perhaps little inclination, to reflect on purpose. Fortunately for us, the Governor of New Jersey in the late 1980s, Thomas Kean, understood the importance of institutional identity and purpose to achieving successful educational outcomes. The Governor offered large grants to colleges and universities throughout the state in order to help them clarify their own distinctiveness, challenging them to 'be bold' and 'innovative' and to rethink institutional mission before the term 'reinventing' was applied to organizations.

The earliest version of *Education for Leadership and Social Responsibility* was born out of an extensive planning process and was awarded $1.8 million for program implementation in 1989. Two years later, due to the vision of Program Officer Bobby Austin, the Kellogg Foundation awarded the comprehensive plan $926,000. We realize that we were very fortunate to have been able to begin this exploration of an educational design with such abundant resources, and that most institutions cannot expect that kind of a start. One of the reasons for writing this book — while acknowledging that early support — is to share the things we have learned so others may not have to spend lots of money finding out for themselves.

Early ideas were tested with colleagues over the course of nine years in presentations at professional meetings throughout the country. Some of the most important feedback we received came from exchanges at meetings of the Association for General and Liberal Studies, the Society for College and University Planning, the National Association of Student Personnel Administrators, The Washington Center for Internships, the National Association of Independent Schools, the International

Society for Exploring Teaching Alternatives and at our own conference on New Ways of Learning and Leading held at Wells College. Although the students might not have realized it, we learned a lot from them in our experimental team taught class in 1990.

A serendipitous contact with Max DePree, author of *Leadership is an Art* and *Leadership Jazz* and former President and CEO of Herman Miller Corporation in Michigan, provided an important validation to our emerging concept of inclusive leadership. After a meeting with Max, a network of people in diverse corporate and not-for-profit organizations was established to help promote people-centered approaches to leadership. The Collegial Network still functions as an important source of professional and personal support for us.

Our ideas were nourished as well by several prominent educators who took the time to understand the comprehensive model that we were evolving. Before we had all of the pieces in place (and they are still shifting), words of encouragement and advice from David McLaughlin, then President of the Aspen Institute; from Ted Marchese, Vice-President at the American Association for Higher Education; from Terrell Jones, Deputy Provost at Penn State University; from David Brown, Provost at Wake Forest University and from consultant Gail Chambers were extremely important in keeping us on task. Special gratitude is extended to Bill Toombs, former director of the Penn State Center for the Study of Higher Education.

For the past three years we have been fortunate to have been associated with an experiment at Wells College, building programs and networks to increase understanding of inclusive leadership and to promote leadership opportunities for women. Through these programs, we were able to take what began as a focus on undergraduate education and extend it to non-traditional audiences, including young children and teenagers; corporate women and men; community volunteers; alumnae; entrepreneurs and business people. Although this book continues the focus on the undergraduate experience, much of what we learned at Wells is applicable to the community collaborations that are a necessary part of that experience. We were most fortunate to have the support and colleagueship of Lisa Ryerson, President of Wells College, for the research reported in the book and for the writing of the book. Our staff at Wells — our friends, Karen Kirkpatrick and Meg Rogers — provided the right work environment, and Karen contributed much of her time to the preparation of the manuscript.

We are indebted to the children who inform us in Chapter 2, to their parents for allowing them to participate and granting us permission to use their pictures and to their teachers and principals for letting the 'leadership people' disrupt their schedules. To the artists who invited us into their studios and living rooms for extended periods of time when they might have been working, and spoke to us with great intensity and candor, we offer our admiration and appreciation for what they were able and willing to share. Finally, we are grateful for the support and responsible sociability of our families — Pamela, Christina, Jose Luis, Nicholas, Ian, Carey, Maria and Lee.

The book is divided into two sections. In the first, we explore some theoretical dimensions that have influenced the construction of an education for leadership and social responsibility, including an introduction to the need for inclusive leadership. Findings from research on children, artists and from *Fortune* magazine are used to support a model of higher education that uses the theme of inclusive leadership, the modes of analysis of systems thinking and common good thinking, and collaboration as the dominant working relationship in and out of the classroom.

The second half of the book deals with the practical application of the model to a campus. How does a campus approach the design and implementation of an education for leadership and social responsibility? The focus in all of the chapters is on process and programs. Beginning with the processes of planning and implementation, we move to discussion of programs for faculty development called teachers as leaders/teaching for leadership, the development of an integrated curriculum and co-curriculum, and a consideration of how an education for leadership and social responsibility is to be assessed. In the final chapter, older forms of campus community are rejected in favor of collaborative community, which echoes the themes of an education for leadership and social responsibility.

Though we focus on the framework of an education for leadership and social responsibility to integrate the undergraduate experience and produce desirable educational outcomes, the reader should bear in mind that the details of that particular model are not what is most important. Each institution needs to wrestle with similar questions regarding the purpose, content and process of the education they are delivering. A successful exploration may result in an entirely different subject focus than leadership, although we suspect the social responsibility component will find more endurance. We hope there are valuable insights in this book even for those institutions that will never mention the word leadership but will strive to give their students an education for our collective survival and happiness in the twenty-first century.

Gloria Nemerowicz
Eugene Rosi

Pine Manor College
Chestnut Hill, Massachusetts

August 1996

Part One

Theoretical Dimensions

Chapter 1

Introduction to Inclusive Leadership

We are still a little surprised that we have written a book about leadership. Earlier in our careers, we had both independently — in different institutions and disciplines — rejected the field of *leadership studies* as inherently flawed. Leader connoted exclusivity and hierarchy, and leadership studies focused either on personality traits associated with those who are leaders or on positions defined by power. A leader was something few could be, but many should aspire to be. Like *heroes*, leaders were supposed to be cultural role models. Because they so often fell short, leaders could be dissected for flaws and criticized for failing to provide the necessary leadership to improve conditions.

But much has changed in the world and in the field of leadership studies during the past decade. We now feel part of a movement that seeks to reclaim leadership as a human (not superhuman) process, one that we all have access to and responsibility for. With many others, we have moved from dismissing the study of leadership as a narrow, often elitist, endeavor, to an understanding of the concept's power to promote quality and provide the opportunity for people to define their common good.

Leadership is not and never has been an innocuous concept. Cultural beliefs about leadership have contributed to the explanation and maintenance of inequality in Western society. To the extent that we believe leadership is based on qualities in particular people that are either inborn or are rare and difficult to cultivate, inequalities between those who are or would-be leaders and the rest of us are expected and accepted. If we believe people are born leaders, it is futile to educate for leadership and social responsibility.

The Need for Education for Leadership and Social Responsibility

In this book we are proposing both the need and a method for approaching such an education for leadership and social responsibility. There are two reasons for the urgency we feel to get on with the job.

The first is the need to promote quality in individual lives, in relationships, in institutions, and in the goods and services we produce. The resurgence of interest in leadership in the past ten years is partly connected to the quality movement in the American workplace and to the parallel interest in spirituality and values in corporate life and in other institutions (Deming, 1986; Chappell, 1993). Many have concluded that product or service quality is important both for economic and competitive advantage and for a sense of 'the good life'. Thus we speak of quality of life issues and we search for leadership that will foster higher quality in people and in products.

If we are to make qualitative improvements in our businesses, communities and relationships, our understanding of leadership must change. A culture's assumptions about leadership have much to do with the health of the organizations that heavily influence the lives of individuals. We measure organizational health (Rosen, 1991) by the organization's ability to enhance its members and constituencies and, as a result, produce goods and services that are of high quality. Peter Senge (1990) refers to the creation of the 'learning organization' as the embodiment of this kind of vitality.

A second critical reason to educate for leadership and social responsibility is the need to forge the common good within diversity. Democratic forms of organization depend on the ability to value and utilize individuality while being able to articulate a common good. This is as true of a small work group as it is at the level of national identity. Further, democracies depend on an understanding of the necessity of participation in the process of leadership. When the majority of the population does not vote, democracy is threatened. When the majority of an organization's members and constituencies do not participate in active ways in organizational decisions, the organization (family, club, school, corporation) is weakened (Bellah et al., 1985).

Is the current attention being paid to leadership just another fad? Dozens of popular books signal a general despair about the lack of leadership that we need to see us through our problems. The discussion signals a dissatisfaction with some key aspects of public and private life. Why can't we do better at coming up with solutions to complex political and social problems? Why are interpersonal relationships so fragile and too often destructive? Why do institutions designed to satisfy basic human needs fall short for so many people? How is it possible that American economic pre-eminence is threatened in a global market place?

These felt dissatisfactions, and the fears associated with them, have prompted an interest in finding new ways to improve leadership. The search for leadership is a search to help guide us through rapid and radical social, organizational and technological changes. It is the response of a people accustomed to looking for heroes and supermen to chart the course that we then choose to follow. Of prospective leaders we want to know: 'What's your plan?'; 'How will you change/fix things?'

Many books have been written on the elements of leadership that can help people solve their own or their organization's problems. *Charismatic Leadership* (Conger and Kanungo, 1988), *The New Leaders* (Morrison, 1992), *Visionary Leadership* (Nanus, 1992), *Stewardship* (Block, 1993), *The West Point Way of Leadership* (Donnithorne, 1993), *The Working Leader* (Sayles, 1993), *Authentic Leadership* (Terry, 1993), and *The Courageous Follower* (Chaleff, 1995) are some that have made important contributions to the discussion. Each of these authors sets out to refine and help build a model of leadership that relies on humanistic values and ethical behavior. Several have introduced the idea of leadership as process (Burns, 1978; Senge, 1990; Rost, 1991); a perspective that we seek to carry forward in this book.

The process of leadership propels people to find and solve problems, to identify their common good, to seek more information — to learn. The process is social and interactive, by definition. Therefore, the traditional, impenetrable boundary between leaders and followers is of little use. All are engaged in a leadership process.

This book goes beyond the current literature in the belief that we can and must ready people for the process of leadership earlier in their lives and in a way that is integrated with the rest of their development. Although there are some corporate and community attempts to develop leadership, they cost billions of dollars in consumer and taxpayer money, they are selective in who is able to receive the development, and they are probably less effective than early learning. As Conger has suggested (1992), such leadership training is often an alternative to true change from within an organization, change that would take longer than a five-day training week and might result in the cultivation of broad-based leadership at many levels within the organization. Skill building doesn't often change world views, a necessary component for true organizational or personal change (Sayles, 1993).

People need to be prepared to enter the community and the workplace with expectations for their roles in the process of leadership. We are not interested in producing 200 or 2000 more leaders. We are interested in producing people who understand the principles that underlie what we call 'inclusive leadership' — understand it to be a process that they have a right to, and will expect to, participate in. Education for leadership and social responsibility is not the domain of the corporate, religious, military or academic elite — the traditional training grounds. It belongs embedded in the schools, public and private, elementary and secondary, and in higher education.

The Current State of Education for Leadership

One of the things that has struck us in our work with secondary and primary schools is how little conscious attention is paid to teaching for leadership. One might assume that in a democracy, 'where people get the leaders they deserve', there would be more than a historical, 'great man' approach to leadership which relates the stories that have shaped our view of leadership. (See Gardner, 1995, for the importance of stories in framing issues.) Leadership is avoided as a curriculum and outcome goal for several reasons.

There is still much confusion and debate about the meaning of leadership. How can one teach about a concept without some agreement on its components? There are those who believe that leadership can't be taught, either because it is an inborn trait or an ability developed through breeding, not the domain of the public schools. Some educators argue that leadership is knowledge-based and a good liberal education is all that is necessary to produce leaders. Others see leadership development as the province of non-teaching personnel: in colleges it would reside with student life staff; in secondary schools, with extra-curricular activities such as clubs, scouting, church groups and sports.

Although many college catalogues include 'preparation for leadership' among the goals of the education at that particular institution, few explicitly address the issue of leadership in a systematic, integrated and comprehensive way. Instead it is assumed that if one participates in the life of the college, perhaps taking a course or two about leadership when available, the capacity and the desire for leadership will result.

In 1987, 94 institutions of higher education were included in the *Leadership Education Source Book* (Clark, Freeman and Britt, 1987). At that time, most campus leadership development efforts fell into one of two categories. Most prevalent were those within the area of student life that were designed to develop personal attributes and skills assumed to be associated with good leadership. Academic courses were far more rare and were disparate and typically career-oriented. Most courses, directed at would-be managers, included an examination of leadership styles and business decision-making. Significant exceptions were single courses exploring the psychology and politics of leadership.

By the early 1990s, about 200 universities (of the more than 3000 two- and four-year institutions in the US) were described as offering courses in leadership, joined by a number of new programs (Clark and Freeman, 1990; Freeman and King, 1992). Most notable was the founding, at the University of Richmond, of the first and only undergraduate degree program in leadership studies. In addition, five small to mid-sized, private institutions reported college-wide approaches to educating for leadership. Also at this time (1993), the *Journal of Leadership Studies* was established to 'serve as a forum for the expression of current thought, technique, theory, ideas, issues, trends, and innovations in the field.' From 1993 to 1996, 17 articles — about 14 per cent of the total published in the journal — addressed curriculum and teaching about leadership.

With some notable and encouraging exceptions, the typical college approach to leadership is still through the division of Student Life, which on most American campuses is not well-integrated with Academic Affairs, is considered extra-curricular, is targeted to small numbers of students, namely those who are in leadership positions on campus, and is focused on management issues, i.e., how to run a meeting, manage your time, or give a speech.

Although we are seeing more attention paid to leadership at the college level, the successful integration of leadership into the educational experience has not been accomplished. Furthermore, though many institutions may agree that leadership is a desirable outcome, there is considerable variation in the conception of leadership. We believe that most people complete their formal education with little sense of personal identification with the concept of leadership, little sense of their responsibility to participate in leadership, and no appreciation that it is their responsibility to cultivate leadership within their organizations.

The Context for Leadership in the Twenty-first Century

An essential part of any effort to educate for leadership and social responsibility is an attempt to inventory the realities of the twenty-first century, when the leadership will be applied. Clearly the desired characteristics of leadership will be shaped by perceptions of the anticipated challenges in communities, politics, families and work. Constructing an inventory of twenty-first century realities is a valuable exercise for educators, as it stimulates an examination of beliefs and understandings about the new millennium and, consequently, reveals assumptions about how students need to be prepared for it.

What follows is a list of realities, already part of our everyday existence, that will become more pronounced in the next millennium. They derive from the profound concerns that have been raised about the prospects in the future for: the physical viability of our planet; the destructive as well as constructive potentials of our known and future technologies; persistent intergroup tensions and inequalities; and the inability of public and private institutions to serve human needs. While the realities we discuss below do not exhaust the possibilities, we assume their importance must be acknowledged as we shape an understanding of leadership education.

1   Organizational, community, and global *pluralism* is an accepted and increasingly valued reality of life. The objective of discovering and valuing diversity in people, cultures and ideas occupies a significant portion of community, academic and corporate attention. Further, for the healthy individual there is a need to be aware of and be comfortable with one's own cultural and gender identity in order to appreciate the diversity that others offer.

2   The troublesome side of pluralism is the reality that difference is often the basis for structured *inequality*. Inequalities are created and maintained by the economies and the ideologies of nations, organizations and communities. They are at the heart of *conflict* in organizational and global arenas. *Economic scarcity*, and its manifestation in un- and under-employment, malnutrition and war, is a reality that impacts the lives of individuals and whole countries. The inability to provide economic participation to all members of our communities has devastating consequences for the survival of democratic organizations and for the growth of healthy leadership.

3   Organizing diverse people into groups that live, grow, explore, produce, reproduce and solve problems is increasingly likely to be done using more horizontal, *flatter forms of organization*. In addition, these groups are linked in *networked* relations with one another in forms that are still emerging. As it grows horizontally, the networked organization creates webs of interdependencies among its members.

   Traditional, pyramidal, bureaucratic structures that rely on hierarchy for order and conformity are becoming obsolete (Miles and Snow, 1986). The rational model of human behavior, especially rational decision-making — upon which this organizational model is based, is being questioned (Sayles, 1993).

Hierarchy can no longer control the flow of communication, the chain of command is often difficult to identify, and the effectiveness of top-down, command and control leadership is questionable.

Horizontal organizations assume a more holistic approach to their members and to the work of the organization, rather than the more narrow, role-specific approach of the bureaucratic system. Instead of conformity to a status quo, people in these new organizations expect that creativity and change will occur as a result of interaction among members. Creativity and improvisation from all parts of the organization are encouraged. Participants are defined as capable of understanding the system and are entitled to information.

4 Within these new structures, *team-based decision-making*, production, and accountability are replacing reliance on the individual. *Collaboration* and *cooperation* are replacing competition as the primary relation within and among organizations and communities. There is increasing need for awareness of *interdependence*, the limits of unilateral solutions, and the value of win-win strategies. Clearly, in order for these new forms to be successful there must be open opportunity for members to participate.

5 New organizations, new relationships, and the value of pluralism are all related to the reality of *accelerating, complex technologies*. The gap between basic scientific discovery and its application continues to narrow, making the consequences of choice more momentous. Today's technology can contribute to both a sense of individual powerlessness as well as a tremendous increase in the availability of resources at one's fingertips.

The perception of technology as a quick fix for our pressing social problems allows a false sense of security to mask the reality of technology itself as a problem involving the need for human choice. Many still perceive technological development as a gradual, controllable process that provides time for experts to make the 'right' choices. Actually, the development is often exponential, with decision-making impaired by the lag in understanding implications for basic systems and time-honored values.

6 *Democratic values* are increasingly pushing for expression in the twenty-first century. As America continues the experiment to govern a pluralistic population democratically, democratic processes have found a place in Eastern Europe, in the republics

of the former Soviet Union and, in the face of great resistance, in China. While there is no guarantee that democracy abroad will prevail and while the euphoria of 1989–90 has vanished, democratic values and processes continue to provide a powerful benchmark. The values include: equal opportunity for participation in the life of the organization or society by all members; honoring the dignity of individual human life; freedom of expression of opinions and access to information; and the application of the principles of justice. In American workplaces, schools, communities and families, the strain to fulfill the promise of democracy is evident (Bellah et al., 1991; Barber, 1992).

Decentralization and the Common Good

Whether or not one values these six realities, they are with us in both public and private ways, through every aspect of our lives. Our families, schools, governments, religions, communities and businesses feel the impact of pluralism and the potential for inequality and conflict. Our institutions are likely to be experimenting with flatter organizational forms to get their jobs accomplished, and, in the context of pluralism and potential conflict, they will be relying on collaboration and team-based decision-making. Increasingly, people will expect to be a part of many teams, will expect to be heard and be required to listen, and expect to never stop learning, teaching and taking risks. Hopefully, much of this will be supported with reference to democratic values, rights and responsibilities.

Each of these realities — in our personal, political and organizational life — supports a tendency toward decentralization, autonomy and heterogeneity. From the break up of the Soviet Union to the successful General Motors Saturn plants, from the modern American family, to educational compacts and charter schools, there is increasing stress on independent definition of outcomes, local decision-making and control of the process, the valuing of difference and distinctiveness, and a reliance on increasingly sophisticated technologies to get the job done.

The first reality, *pluralism*, is a value-neutral concept that seeks to describe 'the many.' When it is applied to human groupings, the basis of classification is some social category with meaning to the history and identity of people. But, of course, human identity has never been value-neutral. Although this country was founded on the principles of democracy and pluralism, the struggle to value and utilize differences productively continues. Tendencies toward ethnocentrism — seeing one's own group as 'the best' — are as true in modern corporate America as they are in high schools. We know that group pride, patriotism and loyalty are positive emotions for the preservation of groups. The same elements that hold smaller groups together, however, lead to 'in-group/ out-group' thinking associated with prejudice, competition, rivalry, hoarding, domination and overt conflict. How do we preserve and honor group differences while drawing larger circles of inclusion?

The second reality — *flatter organizations* — also encourages decentralization. As opposed to the newer, flat organizational model, the traditional hierarchy that we have become accustomed to appears very neat. It is part of a rational model of behavior whose organizational component, the bureaucracy, is highly centralized. The classic work of Max Weber (1947) outlines the dimensions of bureaucratic organization and links the development of bureaucratic forms to the dominance of rationality as the desired and actual model of human behavior. Weber points out the need for rationality in social systems which have converted from small, intimate communities to large, differentiated urban centers. Given the high degree of specialization within bureaucracies, people enter their roles credentialed and are differentially rewarded based on the scarcity of their credential or talent as well as the responsibility of their position. Emphasis is on position, not people.

Bureaucracy promotes predictability, impersonality and control of information, thus bringing order to what might be the chaotic mix of masses of different people. In some ways, living and working and relating within bureaucratic structures relieves people and their leaders of the need to define a common good. The structure does that for them. The common good is managing the bureaucratic system, letting the rules of the system work, and, at the bottom line, keeping the system going. Such a common good does not deal with human purpose beyond the reason for which the bureaucracy was created.

Flatter structures push responsibilities farther into the organization, to the people who actually do the work. There is less traditional managing of subordinates by superiors and therefore more leadership opportunity. Individual work groups, teams, learning groups, coordinating groups are given more autonomy to define the job and how it will be done; to locate resources and organize to do the job; and ultimately to evaluate the results.

Flatter structures eliminate close supervision and often create autonomous cells within the larger structure. While many applaud the increasing reliance on teams — in the workplace, in classrooms, as a model of family life, and for communities — for the spirit of equality and collaboration that they engender, we need to be cautious of the tendency of teams to lose sight of an overarching common good of which they are a part. The same forces at work in the arena of pluralism are at work whenever groups are created with identity and special purpose. The challenge for leadership, at all levels of organizations, in families, corporations and nations, is to create the conditions for inclusion of these autonomous units into a larger enterprise.

The influence on decentralization of *technology* has interested social scientists since the mass production of the automobile. We are accustomed to people being physically decentralized from their families, their communities and their workplaces. Can families hold together and serve the needs of their members for identity, emotional and economic support and Thanksgiving dinner when they may live and/or work thousands of miles apart? Can work organizations thrive in the age of the 'virtual office'? Can communities educate the children of families whose members are physically absent from the community either permanently or for long periods of time?

Through the information revolution, people are at once able to communicate with millions of people they have never met; to decentralize their engagement with others to very specific topics; and to work, play and shop quite alone with their computer keyboards. The possibilities presented by technology have altered public discourse. There is little room to decide *if* something should exist in the realm of possibilities. Rather, if it is technologically possible, it *will* exist and the discussion, if any, will have to do with the choice of application. While technology clearly offers tremendous advantages for the quality of human life, people are disconnected from the production of technological devices, which is left to technical experts, and often from the decisions about application, which are left to moral or legal experts.

Democratic values continue to undergird the rights and responsibilities of the individual in relationship to government and to other citizens. They honor the individual as 'endowed with unalienable rights'. While they put emphasis on individual rights, in the best democratic systems they do so in the context of the collective and with the purpose of making the collective enterprise work. Individual rights are balanced with group level responsibilities. Often, democratic rights and responsibilities sit uncomfortably with other organizational goals and centralized control emerges. We have often heard 'this is not a democracy' from classroom teachers, parents and bosses, in response to complaints by participants. Democratic values are often overridden by organizational values that call on certain leadership positions to give direction, to impose order and meaning: i.e., the teacher, parent, boss 'knows best,' or he or she may not always be right but is the teacher, parent or boss 'so you better do as you are told'. Agreement on democratic values that honor the individual and at the same time require participation in a larger enterprise is the best foundation we have for locating the common good.

At the turn of the last century, sociologists and others were concerned with the impact of the Industrial Revolution and urbanization on our social institutions. How, they asked, would a society characterized by an increasingly specialized division of labor and by differences in ethnicity, religion and social class, be held together to function as a whole? Most influential was Emile Durkheim's analysis (1933) that 'interdependence of unlike parts' was to be the social glue in heterogeneous societies, replacing the glue of familiarity that characterized more traditional, homogeneous societies. Interdependence implies an equality of dependency that is rarely apparent. It implies an equality of value in the eyes of the other. One does not have to look far to see evidence that some people — those living in cardboard boxes, those without medical insurance, those working at minimum wage or not working at all, those who do not fit cultural standards of mental and physical appropriateness — are more dependent than others. Interconnectedness conceals levels of (inter)dependence.

The division of labor and the revolution in production that transformed our lives at the beginning of this century understandably led to concern for the integration of society and for the ability of social systems to hold together in the future. The post-industrial future has been upon us for at least the last 30 years. The most important challenge facing leadership today — at all levels within organizations, communities, and families — is creating conditions that allow the members to manifest their individual and group level differences while at once defining their common good and finding ways to pursue it.

The Common Good and Inclusive Leadership

The preceding discussion makes clear the need for links among smaller groups of people within a larger common enterprise. The smaller group may be the children in the family, a particular nation, an interest group within a community, an ethnic group within a nation or a work team in a company. We have said that it is the job of leadership to help diverse people define their own common good and find means to pursue it. In subsequent chapters we will learn more about the kind of leadership that can do this. Before we turn to some new sources for more insight into leadership, let us review the assumptions we are making.

The traditional concept and practice of leadership is not well suited to deliver what is needed. Because it is defined by position in a hierarchy, traditional leadership is achieved through possession of credentials which provide access to the position. In addition, the position demands, and others expect, that the leader will do the defining of purpose and will solve the problems at hand. If he/she cannot, a new leader will be found. The traditional relationship between leaders and followers is one of inequality. Distinct differences in character, breeding, personality, intellect or other traits separate the few leaders and the many followers. Most followers are assumed to be basically lazy and motivated by narrow self-interest. The few good leaders that are necessary are produced primarily by select institutions.

It is unimaginable that traditional leaders would engage in the processes that would result in inclusivity and common good thinking. Communication between leaders and followers is formal, prescribed by hierarchical rules of command and custom. Communication is not spontaneous, nor is it two-way; control of information is a base of power. Since information can be dangerous in the wrong hands, it is shared selectively. Consultation occurs only among certain positions; too much consultation will be interpreted as a sign of the leader's inability to make decisions and lead. Ethics, which can unite groups of people around principles, are often seen as incompatible with strong leadership, which sometimes relies on secrecy, deception and favoritism to accomplish goals.

In contrast, a new model of leadership has emerged to offer alternative conceptualizations and assumptions that will influence leadership. Many are working to craft the new model, and the language we have to describe it is still in flux (see citations, pp. 4–5). We call the new model *inclusive leadership*.

This kind of leadership is not dependent on position; it is expected to be manifest throughout an organization in relationships among people. Leadership is evaluated qualitatively by how people are working together to define and pursue their common good. Leaders and followers mentor, coach and learn together. Followers are active participants in the process, shaping and drawing out leadership when it is needed. In this model, leadership derives from basic human characteristics that are cultivatable in people. Among the characteristics are creativity, curiosity, empathy and cooperation. Nearly everyone can acquire the propensity for each of these behaviors, which are not inborn.

In systems characterized by inclusive leadership, information is systematically sought and freely shared. Two-way communication is critical, with an emphasis on the skill of listening. Value is placed on democratic processes, on honesty and fairness, respect for the individual, and responsibility and accountability. Inclusive leadership is socially responsible leadership, inclusive of many diverse people united by the search to define and act on common good goals. The absence of stark differences between leaders and followers in terms of any social characteristics or preconceived qualifications promotes a sense of familiarity, reciprocity and equality between leaders and followers. Leadership is not a mystery.

These broad brush strokes illustrate that by definition inclusive leadership must involve people in creating their own futures and in solving problems in order to increase well-being and assure our collective future. Sound like a tall order? It is. But it is precisely the order given to liberal education.

Listening to the Voices of Children, Business and Artists

Clearly, we need to know more about this powerful concept before we begin crafting the education that will help people create and use it. In order to provide more clarity to our thinking about inclusive leadership, we turn to three voices with very different experiences but, perhaps surprisingly, with similar perspectives when it comes to leadership.

First we will speak with those who are learning the cultural rules and expectations about leadership — children. We turn to children to better understand the messages we adults transmit about leadership and thus to better understand our own thinking. We also turn to them as consultants about how leadership might be done better, to achieve more cooperation and better results. The importance of listening to the ideas of children has been convincingly argued by Howard Gardner: 'Education that takes seriously the ideas and intuitions of the young child is far more likely to achieve success than education that ignores these views, either considering them to be unimportant or assuming they will disappear on their own' (Gardner, 1991:248).

Next, the voice of the business community will be heard through an analysis of *Fortune* magazine. Is inclusive leadership relevant to the contemporary workplace? When educating for leadership and social responsibility, are we also educating for the real world of work?

Table 1.1: Comparing traditional leadership with inclusive leadership

Traditional Leadership	Inclusive Leadership
Identified by position in a hierarchical structure. Relies on rational model of human behavior: depersonalized relationships, predictability, and efficiency.	A quality of the interaction of people. Not dependent on position — expectation that it will come throughout organization.
Leadership is evaluated by how leader is doing at solving problems. Leaders provide solutions and answers.	Leadership is evaluated by how people are working together to define and improve their common good, solve problem, etc. Leader as mentor, guide, empowering others, learner and teacher.
Distinct differences between leaders and followers: character, personality, and breeding. Followers are assumed to be motivated solely by self-interest and are lazy.	Leaders and followers have an interdependent relationship. Followers are active participants in the process of leadership.
The province of a few (good men). Produced by select institutions.	Based on human characteristics that are teachable/learnable: empathy, creativity, cooperation and curiosity.
Communication between leaders and followers is infrequent and formal. Little consultation necessary or desirable. Information is controlled and retained as source of power.	Information is systematically sought and and freely shared. Communication is critical, with a stress on listening.
Ethics often incompatible with strong leadership which often must rely on secrecy, deception and payoffs.	Values democratic processes, honesty and shared ethics. Seeks a common good within diversity.

Finally, we will hear from those who engage regularly and creatively in processes of problem finding and solving, and in perfecting the quality of their work. They work collaboratively as well as independently to seek new ways to express the common human condition. These leaders, rarely viewed as such, are called artists. We believe their knowledge of the process of creativity will help clarify the process of leadership.

The perspectives of these groups will help us refine the necessary approach and elements of an education for leadership and social responsibility which we will examine in the second part of this book.

Chapter 2

Learning about Leadership from Children

The most important thing about being a leader is to get the right people to help you (Tracey, 5th grade).

If you want to be a leader you have to learn about politics, the Soviet Union, reading, math (up to 100) and how to tie your shoes (William, 4th grade).

There's never been a woman President, for some odd reason (Amy, 4th grade).

Although this book proposes a model of education for leadership and social responsibility that is focused primarily on higher education, we begin our exploration of the ingredients of the model with young children. In order to shape an effective education for older students, we thought it necessary to under-stand the assumptions and beliefs about leadership held by young children.

Children mirror the reality of the culture in which they are raised, with all the complexities of race, gender and class reflected in their opinions. They are often able to 'tell the truth' about social arrangements that adults have come to accept as natural. We believe much can be learned about leadership from young children, including the stereotypes and myths that might impede change. Children can tell us what is wrong through their honest reflection of the messages they are receiving from the adult world.

Children have been studied for their developing ideas about political socialization (Easton and Dennis, 1969), moral development (Kohlberg, 1978; Hoffman, 1981) gender differences (Nemerowicz, 1979; Gilligan, 1982) and other aspects of social development. That there has not been a study of children's perceptions of leadership is an interesting commentary on adult assumptions. Either we have believed that the concept is not well formed in children or that it doesn't have much significance for them.

The Study

During the 1994–95 school year, we talked with 85 fourth and fifth grade students from three schools in upstate New York. This sample, though diverse by design, is not intended to represent the entire American population of children. The sample included a private, age-integrated school; a public school in a rural, largely white, agricultural community; and an urban, multicultural public school. The two public schools were located in areas containing slightly more people below the poverty line than is the average in the state of New York, which, with a poverty rate of 15.3 per cent, ranks above the national median of 13.5 per cent (*Statistical Abstracts of the US*, 1994).

Two instruments were used to collect the data. First, the children were asked to 'draw a picture of leadership'. They were given no further elaboration. The picture was then discussed in interviews lasting about 20 minutes with each child individually. Through discussion of their pictures and several direct questions about leadership, the children were able to use their own words and images to define leadership, demonstrate their feelings about leadership and provide advice for leaders. The children talked freely and most seemed eager and appreciative for the attention and the opportunity to express their opinions.

Key Findings

By 4th grade most children define leadership in terms of the traditional characteristics of control, taking charge and telling others what to do. Furthermore, they do not like this leadership mode nor do they think it is effective.

Figure 2.1: 'It must be fun to be a leader because you get to tell people what to do and when to do it.'

By the time they are 8- or 9-years old, young children have concluded that most leadership is of the authoritarian, hierarchical variety. Children this age receive primary socialization from the home, the media, school and peers. Their experiences with leadership at home, in school and on the playground, as well as the images of current and historical leaders they have absorbed, lead children to consider most leaders to be 'bossy and mean', with little empathy for others.

Children believe more inclusive leadership is desirable. They advise leaders to be less controlling and bossy and more responsive to others.

Figure 2.2: 'Leaders shouldn't have a fit if people do something wrong — nobody's perfect.'

Even though children characterize leadership as traditional and top-down, they appeal to leaders for a more inclusive, respectful leadership that they believe is more effective in getting the job done. According to the children, controlling leadership doesn't work very well because people don't try to do their best when they are not respected and encouraged. Clearly, the children do not like being on the receiving end of authoritarian leadership. They do not understand why leaders feel the need to be bossy and to belittle others.

Less than one-third of the children believe present day leadership is already characterized by an emphasis on teamwork, sharing, letting others choose and cooperation to meet group goals. Most think it is wise to move toward this model.

The leader is seen as different in some noticeable way from the followers and is often physically separated from those being led. Leaders are often depicted as physically out of touch with the people they are leading.

Children use several signs and symbols to denote the power and specialness of the leader. The leader is often depicted as physically separated from others by being elevated to a higher level, by the use of a podium, or by wide distances of space between the leader and others. In 25 per cent of the pictures, the leader is much larger than the other people in the picture. These depictions imply an absence of even the possibility of effective two-way communication. The leader is simply unreachable.

Figure 2.3: 'We the people . . .'

Overwhelmingly, children think we need leaders; without them there would be catastrophic consequences.

The idea of an absence of leadership is unthinkable to most children. There would be dire consequences on every social level. In general, things would be out of control, and there would be 'anarchy' and 'chaos'. In the world there would be no peace and things would 'fall apart'. People would 'go insane', 'get wild', get into fights, and increase the use of violence to solve problems. Further, people would be 'confused', 'not know what to do', 'be disorganized', 'do what they want', and 'not think of other people'. Kids would 'run off' and no learning would take place because there would be no schools. Our country would no longer exist, 'the city would be junk' there would be no laws, no plans and no rules.

According to the children, leaders have a civilizing effect, serving to curb the basic instincts and ruthless individualism of people. There are very few references to the leader as 'evil doer'; rather, evil resides in people and the leader's job is to control it. Possibly the level of fear conjured up by an imagined absence of leaders allows more authoritarianism and controlling behavior by leaders to be tolerated. It is better to be yelled at and told what to do than to have chaos, anarchy and insanity.

A few children believed the absence of leaders would be satisfactory as long as everyone worked together to 'control ourselves' and make decisions.

Children are not cynical about leadership and about the potential for leadership to solve problems.

Figure 2.4: 'Fight for freedom'

They have not given up on the hope that 'leaders will make the world better for people'. For almost half of the sample, leadership is synonymous with problem-solving and taking action. The most frequently mentioned issues that leaders should address are poverty and injustice. Fighting wars and giving directions are also frequently mentioned as actions that involve leadership. Other issues include stopping crime and violence, cultivating friendships and taking care of others, and taking care of the environment.

Children are not receiving supportive messages about their own leadership potential.

Only 36 per cent of the children recall being told by anyone that they would make a good leader. In several cases it was peers, rather than adults, who provided the positive reinforcement of leadership abilities. While adults are sensitive to nurturing academic and social skills in children through praise and encouragement, they are not doing the same encouraging of leadership.

Nearly all children who remember being told by someone that they would make a good leader actually consider themselves to be a leader or aspire to be a leader. The reinforcement by others would seem to be an effective socializer. Of those who do not aspire to leadership, 90 per cent had never been told they would make a good leader.

Figure 2.5: 'Probably everyone could be a leader.'

Half of the children consider themselves to be leaders now or aspire to be leaders.

There is no difference by gender. According to this group, being a leader is a good thing for two reasons. Most prominently, you get to help others. Second, only by being a leader yourself can you escape the control of other leaders and thus achieve some independence.

For those who do not desire leadership, the dangers associated with it are most often mentioned as inhibitors. Leaders get shot, they get yelled at, and, at a minimum, they eventually get criticized. Also, leadership requires sacrifice of other important things like fun, one's family and, according to one child, horseback riding.

Figure 2.6: *'If you follow me, I am the leader.'*

Children can think of more characteristics about themselves that would hinder their own leadership than they can think of characteristics about themselves that would promote their own leadership.

Both boys and girls can name a number of characteristics about themselves that would impede their leadership abilities. Most frequently mentioned are bossiness, laziness, disorganization, a lack of knowledge and a desire to have fun ('do goofy things'). On the positive side, boys value their ability to deal with problems operationally — planning, strategizing, decision-making. Girls value their ability to deal with problems interpersonally and inclusively.

Children believe leadership can be taught.

©1995
nemerowicz & rosi

Figure 2.7: *'If you want to be a leader you need to learn about politics, the Soviet Union, reading, math (up to 100) and how to tie your shoes.'*

They recommend focusing on teaching the values of kindness, honesty and getting along with others. Interestingly, girls more often than boys analyze themselves as already possessing these teachable qualities.

Children obtain their models of leadership primarily from government and politics. Family and school are a second source of examples.

Figure 2.8: 'Leaders are people like Bill Clinton, Jean Luc Picard, my mom.'

President Clinton and former US presidents are the most popular single reference. Teachers, principals and coaches were noted more frequently than family members. There were no references to business leaders and, only by inference, very few references to community leadership. Thus, children use both a distant and a familiar reference for leadership. National political leadership is impersonal, filtered generally through the media and perhaps family discussion. School and family references are more personal, familiar and more authentic.

Coaches and team sports serve as important illustrations of the children's emerging notions of inclusive leadership.

Figure 2.9: 'OK, this is what your doing wrong . . .'

The ease with which children describe coaches as ideal leaders and team sports as ideal cooperative groups was impressive. The new model of leadership often describes leaders as coaches, mentors and facilitators. The children see coaches as caring about everyone, bringing the best out in everyone, mentoring, not yelling and generally as great examples of good leadership.

While there is unanimity that women can be leaders, a significant portion of both boys and girls (42 per cent) could not name a woman leader.

Figure 2.10:   'We never had a woman president for some odd reason.'

For the 52 per cent who could name a woman leader, most referred to a well-known historical or contemporary woman. The impact of the social studies curriculum and the geographical location of the sample in upstate New York was clear in the ability of girls to cite a historical woman figure such as Harriet Tubman (most frequently mentioned), Elizabeth Cady Stanton and Susan B. Anthony. In addition to these three, only Hillary Clinton received more than one mention. Another dozen mentions included sports figures, wives of former Presidents, royal and religious figures.

The second most popular category of reference for women leaders was relatives and school personnel. Only 28 per cent of the children looked in their own backyard for women leaders, citing teachers, coaches and moms.

Both boys and girls depict their own gender as the leader, though boys do so at twice the rate.

When left to their own imagination, both boys and girls picture leaders as in their own gender. This is true nearly unanimously (95 per cent) for boys and in just over half the cases (53 per cent) for girls. Given the overall lack of information about women leaders, it is not surprising that the girls draw anonymous or fictitious women leaders.

Females are overwhelmingly absent as leaders or followers from pictures drawn by boys and are generally present in the girls' pictures.

Females do not usually enter the imagination of boys when they are asked to draw a picture of leadership. In 90 per cent of the pictures drawn by boys, there are no females represented as leaders *or* as followers. In 79 per cent of the girls' pictures, females are present.

29

Advice for Leaders

Perhaps the most compelling data to emerge is the advice that the children had for leaders. The children were asked to think about how current leaders could do a better job, and how leadership could be improved. Their answers fall into five categories: Attitude — Be Humane and Respect Others; Behavior — Help Others; Style — Involve Others; Self-Improvement — Develop Good Habits; and Values — Be Ethical. The children clearly recognize leadership as interactive and interdependent with those one is leading and with larger cultural values. Leadership is not just a matter of perfecting one's own talents.

What follows is the advice of the children, in their own words.

Be Humane and Respect Others

- Think of other people, not just yourself.
- Don't have a fit if people do something wrong — nobody's perfect.
- Don't make slaves of people.
- Correct mistakes without being mean.
- Like people even when they are different.
- When you have to do something, think about how it will affect other people.
- People have rights — don't boss them around.
- Try to understand how little kids feel.
- Don't expect everyone to be just like you.
- Stop trying to be the tough guy.

We should stop the vilence

©1995
nemerowicz & rosi

Figure 2.11:   'We should stop the vilence.'

Help People

- When people are confused, don't leave them confused.
- Let people know they are not all alone with their problems.
- Protect the community.
- Help people make the right choices and find a better way to live.
- Spend more time with people who need their problems solved.
- Try to help the earth more.

Figure 2.12: 'Dounate money for the poor and clouths.'

Involve Others

- Try to create conversation.
- Involve a whole crowd of people in decisions.
- Get shy people into the group.
- Care for what other people say.
- Don't do it all by yourself. Take turns.
- Sometimes a duet is better than a solo.
- Don't have total control.
- Get help from the people.
- Listen to more people. They have good ideas for change. Kids have ideas for cleaning up the planet.
- Let other people talk and you listen.

Figure 2.13: 'Don't do it all by yourself. Take turns.'

Develop Good Work Habits

- When you're learning something, don't quit too early.
- Keep marching till you fall to the ground.
- Learn how to get people to agree with you.
- You can do something faster if you take your time.
- Think things through about five times and always get a second opinion, maybe two or three. Then even if people don't like it, if you think it will help the country (or whatever you are doing) still do it.

- Learn about politics, the Soviet Union, reading, math (up to 100), and how to tie your shoes.
- Pick the right people to help you in whatever you do.
- Control your temper. Have a good time at being a leader.
- Don't get angry at yourself if you can't do well.

Be Ethical

- Don't do what others say if it is bad.
- Be true to the people you are with.
- Do what's fair.
- Don't make rules only for people with money.
- Give to the entire place you are leading.
- Don't talk like TV hosts. Talk like you mean business.

©1995
nemerowicz & rosi

Figure 2.14: 'A leader needs to look out for the rest of the group.'

Application to Educating for Leadership

Although we will return to the wisdom of the children again, what follows are recommendations we can bear in mind when constructing an education for leadership and social responsibility for any age level. The recommendations are applicable to social systems beyond the school as well. As the list is reviewed, its application to families, communities, workplaces and governments should be remembered.

- *Make the topic of leadership a more direct part of curriculum and conversation.*

In the schools, adopt a school-based approach to teaching for leadership based on the community's definition of the elements of inclusive leadership. Leadership will not be developed if the concept is a mysterious thing, seldom spoken about, and reserved for those who seem to possess superhuman qualities. Use the word leadership to describe behaviors that reflect inclusive leadership characteristics so that children connect their own behavior with leadership. Thus, when a child is humane, respectful of the feelings of others, includes others, is persistent and deliberate, problem-finds and problem-solves, and makes ethical judgments, that piece of behavior should be explicitly recognized as contributing to good leadership.

- *Introduce the idea of a 'common good'.*

Provide opportunities for children to think about the common good and how to achieve the best outcomes for the common good. Raising questions about the common good at once raises questions about the parts of the system involved — thus common good thinking is tied to systems thinking. Like writing, speaking, listening and critical thinking, common good thinking is a skill that requires repeated opportunities for practice, peer review, revision and improvement. This will often take the form of brainstorming sessions, the analysis of appropriate case studies derived from children's literature and media, as well as current and historical events.

- *Increase collaborative learning opportunities and reinforce the association between leadership and problem-finding and solving.*

The method of collaborative learning is an ideal tool for the teaching of leadership. Within the process of collaboration, several elements necessary for leadership are present: team work, shared decision-making, common good thinking, appreciation and utilization of diversity, listening and communicating. As the group takes responsibility for the collective outcome, it also takes responsibility for the success of each individual in the group.

Problem-finding is part of the necessary creativity of leadership. Are children encouraged to find and articulate problems both within the organization of their education as well as in the larger community or is such behavior seen as trouble-making and challenging to the adult authorities? We need to rethink how much problem-finding and solving responsibilities are taken over by the adults and whether more might be left to the students to enhance their learning.

- *Analyze the way decisions are made in school and in the family.*

Talk about the kinds of leadership that are used and whether there might be changes to get more people, including the children, involved. A systems analysis of the school, the classroom or the community is an exercise even young children can do. What are the parts? What are the decisions? How are they made? Such inquiry has the secondary benefit of allowing children to talk with the leaders and increase their exposure to leadership at all levels of an organization.

- *Involve adults — teachers and parents — as partners in learning with the child.*

The development of leadership is dependent on the community in which the leadership is to be exercised. If we are to educate for leadership, the adults in the child's world must enter the learning process in an active way as learners as well as teachers.

Computers provide a great opportunity for this kind of shared learning as technology has equalized much of the knowledge difference between the generations. Another opportunity is in shared concern for community problems such as the environment, a community building project, or volunteer work in the community in which both adults and children participate as peers.

- *Point out examples of leadership in the world beyond politics and government and provide opportunities for children to experience and practice leadership.*

To undo the child's idea that leadership is an all consuming activity, help children identify leadership in communities and in all occupations to reinforce the belief that leadership is not incompatible with other things they might want to do. This calls for a demystification of leaders to reveal their common humanity and the multiplicity of their life interests. It also leads to consideration of the responsible leadership components of nearly all roles in life. What are the leadership components of being a scientist, a dad or an ice skater? These kinds of considerations dispel the idea that leadership exists as a separate and special social role to be occupied by separate and special people.

Provide access to leaders of all kinds and at all levels of organizations. Demonstrate that leadership is found not just at the top of organizations. It is a quality of people and is found in relationships whenever people work and play and learn together. Leaders are regular people with problems and weaknesses. They have the same characteristics the children note as impediments to their own leadership potential: a desire to have fun, to have a family, or sometimes be lazy or bossy or messy.

Implement the idea of intermittent leadership, leadership that does not stick to the individual, so one might be a leader in one situation and a follower in another. Do not identify only a few children as 'the leaders'. When this is done, children get the idea that leadership is something that is best left to a chosen few that does not include them. Make it clear that we all have the responsibility and capability for being leaders sometimes.

- *Develop in children an awareness of the importance of active, participatory followership.*

Explore the relationships between leaders and followers so children appreciate the interdependency. The teaching of social responsibility can be framed in demonstrations of the responsibility of followers to support, criticize or help change leadership.

- *Discuss with the individual child his or her leadership potential.*

Dispel the idea that there is a set of personality characteristics that leaders are born with. Emphasize the positive qualities the child has. Even if the child does not like to give speeches, he or she still has leadership potential based on such qualities as being a good listener, being creative, being patient and kind, and being smart at figuring out how to involve other people in decisions.

- *Provide more information about the leadership contributions of women in all arenas.*

An education for leadership is necessarily joined with an education to diversity. Leadership relies on community definitions, team work, shared values and common good thinking. The greatest challenge to leadership in the twenty-first century is to discover, enjoy and utilize diversity while pursuing a common good.

Both boys and girls need information about women leaders that goes beyond the famous to include those women in business, the community, and political arenas who are helping to redefine the nature of leadership. The total absence of women as participants in the drawings of boys signals a need to pay more attention to how boys are conceptualizing the roles of women and the compatibility of women with leadership. Increasing the opportunities for all children to take various leadership roles in and out of school should help boys feel more comfortable with the idea of women as leaders beyond the family and school.

- *Reinforce interpersonal skills for their importance to leadership.*

Those children who already demonstrate these skills, particularly girls, need reinforcement that their interpersonal skills, abilities to negotiate conflict, interest in including everyone, and ability to listen well are considered important for good leadership. Boys especially need to cultivate these skills and, by reference to the needs of the contemporary business and political arenas, to increase the value placed on them. Examples of the need for these skills are abundant in historical and contemporary issues. Children would find it encouraging that interpersonal and team building skills are considered by businesses to be the most significant areas in need of development for their employees.

- *Allow time for coaches and teachers to reflect on what and how they are teaching about leadership.*

These important socializers may not appreciate the impact they have on children's developing notions of leadership, an impact that goes well beyond sports and the classroom. Teachers and coaches need to consider the messages they are transmitting both by what they teach and how they teach it. Current teacher education curricula pay little attention to the teacher as a leader who is teaching for leadership.

peɑse on earth

Figure 2.15: 'People want to be leaders to make the world good.'

Are the ideas about leadership that children hold far-fetched and unrealistic? Will an education for leadership and social responsibility that takes these ideas seriously ill-prepare students for the 'real world'? In the next chapter we visit the real world of business in order to help answer these questions.

Chapter 3

Learning about Leadership from the World of Work

From *Fortune* magazine:

> Find out what people are thinking, let them design solutions, get out of the way and let them put solutions into practice.

> Unbridled individualism can foster not only personal opportunity and upward mobility, but also civic complacency and collective decline.

> On average, a 10 per cent increase in workforce education level led to an 8.6 per cent gain in total factor productivity, while a 10 per cent rise in the value of capital equipment increased productivity only 3.4 per cent.

> Make the company a true democracy, a place run on trust and freedom, not fear.

In Chapter 1, we posited some trends that we expect will dominate the twenty-first century and we outlined the ingredients of inclusive leadership that should influence an education for leadership. In Chapter 2, in their own language, young children validated the essence and much of the specifics of inclusive leadership as an ideal. At the same time, the children revealed that inclusive leadership is not the reality they experience in their world, nor is it what they perceive to exist in the larger world. Now we need to know if the principles of inclusive leadership make sense within the context of contemporary American business and within the larger organizational world of work.

Students and their parents often pay large amounts of money to obtain an education beyond the high school level. They are motivated to do so by many factors, chief among them being the belief that their education will result in better paying jobs and more opportunities in the world of work.[1] It is important therefore, for practical reasons as well as reasons of social responsibility, that colleges and universities provide their graduates with skills, information and capacities that are necessary for that success. We recognize that the world of work is not the only arena of importance to people. Later in this chapter we provide parallels between the themes and needs of the institution of work and the themes and needs of family, community and politics.

Content Analysis of *Fortune* Magazine

In order to explore the fit between the principles of inclusive leadership and the issues that are of concern in the contemporary business workplace, we conducted a content analysis of *Fortune* magazine. While not the exclusive voice for American business, with a biweekly circulation of nearly one million the magazine is consulted regularly as an index of important business issues.

Fifty-two issues of *Fortune* magazines constituted the sample, representing every issue from June 1991 through May 1992 and every issue from January through December 1995. Eighty-seven articles were reviewed for their relevance to the characteristics of inclusive leadership we have suggested. Articles that discussed leadership, workplace organization, social responsibility, and the real and desired characteristics of employees were counted and analyzed for content.

Thirty eight of the issues (78 per cent) contained articles which fell into our areas of interest. Of the 87 articles reviewed, all but seven (91 per cent) were supportive of the principles of inclusive leadership. The seven critical articles appeared in the 1995 issues of the sample, indicating some possible cynicism about the viability of 'a new kind of leadership'. We divided the articles into four themes, representing clusters of ingredients for inclusive leadership. The categories are:

1. Values: The Foundation for the Process of Work

These articles speak about the importance of guiding principles or beliefs that underlie the process of work and reflect a common understanding of the purpose and spirit of the organization. Increasingly, businesses are recognizing that without common beliefs and understandings, it is impossible for people to cooperate, to trust each other and to care about what they are doing.

Businesses, many of them major corporations, are identifying 'soft values', which include creating a 'caring environment' that supports the well-being of the employee, the customer, and the surrounding community of which the business is a part. The values rest on a belief in the basic dignity of individuals and the need for individuals to build trusting relationships.

According to *Fortune* magazine, 50 per cent of companies in the US now have a mission statement of some sort.[2] In addition to being articulated and in most cases written down, the values and ethical principles that guide business behavior are often described as part of a company's 'culture.' Employees, boards of directors, customers, suppliers, and surrounding communities are all made aware of the norms, beliefs, symbols and values of the 'corporate culture.' In many cases they are also made aware of their role in creating, sustaining and modifying the culture.

Culture serves as the unifying framework within which business decisions and human relations policies are formulated. Agreement on the basic parameters of the culture, inclusion within the culture, and the ability to partake of the benefits of the culture insure that the organization of people will remain 'robust.' Having a 'robust culture' is noted as a characteristic that defines the most admired companies. Moreover, according to Tom Peters, corporate cultures that put their three constituencies — shareholders, customers, employees — on the same plane, as opposed to putting shareholders first, do the best for shareholders.[3]

As businesses have been challenged to change rapidly and often radically in order to survive, the emphasis on values and culture as a stabilizing force is clear. The articles suggest that core values are necessary to hold together work organizations that can no longer count on traditional hierarchy and authority to command conformity. As changes such as 'downsizing,' outsourcing, and autonomous work groups mean that fewer people remain located and loyal to one central work space, people need values that transcend one particular organization. The business values described in the articles — democracy, respect, social responsibility, fairness, trust, egalitarianism — are generalizable to the best human relationships.

Many of the articles talk about the 'emotional' life of the company which is manifest in sensitivity to the feelings of employees and sometimes customers and suppliers as well. The ability to 'listen' to how people are feeling, to mentor and coach are considered important skills. The emotional life of the company proceeds from the emotional health of the individuals associated with the company, to the relationships they form with one another in common pursuit of the company's goals. The health of those relationships is ultimately the health of the business. Healthy relationships allow people to 'take risks,' 'be more creative,' give and receive support, and be more accountable.

2. *Preparing the Participants: Energizing, Empowering, and Educating*

A belief in the ability of people to 'do the right thing' for the good of the company is reflected in articles that proclaim the need for an 'empowered,' 'autonomous' work force. Other articles prescribe how such a work force can be achieved. Trust is often mentioned as the fuel that powers the engine of human capital development. Trust is engendered by a commitment to shared company values and a sense of the common good.

According to these articles, expectations for behavior in the workplace have changed. Rather than a passive, rule-obeying work force, guided by narrow specializations and areas of responsibility, today's workers are expected to be involved in decision-making, in generating ideas, in problem-solving and problem-finding. Much of this is to be done directly with customers and suppliers outside the immediate work environment.

Peter Senge's idea of a 'learning organization' (1990) is apparent in many of the descriptions of companies striving to create environments of 'renewal,' 'growth' and 'learning how to unlearn' and where 'people can reach their dreams'. According to one article, 'learning is replacing control'. People are seen as capable of continuous learning and innovation if they are provided with the support and the information they need. Businesses must 'turn employee's knowledge (human capital) into a shared, firm-wide asset' (structural capital).[4]

In order to be effective decision-makers and informed risk-takers, employees at all positions within the company need access to information. Information is a critical ingredient in the process of learning. Several articles discuss the need for widespread access to information throughout an organization. Some of the information now available to most employees, such as financial reports, used to be considered dangerous in the hands of anyone other than a few trusted high level managers. These articles suggest that trust based on a common set of values has replaced suspicion on both sides. It is presumed that the common good is as recognizable to line workers as to managers, even when the company's common good is served by the loss of jobs.

In addition to access to information, the importance of the communication skill of listening is underscored in order to insure that ideas and needs are heard and responded to. Managers are advised to 'unleash the workers', 'trust your employees', 'energize others', 'liberate your employees', 'give people voice and responsibility', and 'get out of the way'.

3. The Process of Work: Collaborations and Teams

These articles go far beyond the truism that people need to be able to get along with others in order to work effectively. Rather, they speak of both the need for and effectiveness of teams and collaborative relationships.

The use of teams to energize and free the individual is supported by the organizational values of interdependence, cooperation, risk-taking, respect and trust. Teams that are based on a commitment to a quality outcome, that engender trust, and are given broad responsibility for the process of production are characterized as the best work processes for individuals and the company. Teams will get the best out of individuals.

The articles stress the importance of conceptualizing 'fluid boundaries' for teams both within and outside of the company. An important corporate value at GE is 'boundarylessness'.[5] The team concept goes beyond a workplace group to encompass all parties in the process of work. It is necessary that consumers, suppliers, other community groups, and in some cases even competitors be related to as respected partners. Part of the challenge of this systems thinking is to define anew the web of relationships which have been previously ignored or taken for granted. Is the customer always right? Is the supplier always trying to cheat you? Are your competitors never your allies? Managers or 'team leaders' are advised, 'don't be afraid to admit ignorance', 'learn to truly share power', 'be patient', 'organize employees in innovative and flexible ways'.

The picture that emerges is of teams and work groups that are constantly forming, dissolving, and reforming to get the job done. The employee's vision of the process of work is expanded to include many constituencies to whom the employee must be sensitive and with whom the team must find ways of communicating.

Rather than suppressing the individual, the team process is believed to allow for the 'discovery of self and of others' and most importantly of what can be created when people work openly and honestly with one another within a framework of common values. There are indeed 'softer values' involved in 'building a team, sharing ideas, and exciting others'.

4. Organizational Form: Flatter Structures

There seems to be little controversy about the organizational form necessary to carry out the objectives of modern businesses. The traditional hierarchical model is associated with both values and behaviors that are no longer seen as desirable. The rational, predictable, authority-based hierarchy, characterized by top-down flow of directives, control of information, and impersonal relationships, does not serve the goals of the modern organization. A hierarchical organization does not facilitate the empowerment of workers, nor does it support the use of cross-functional, collaborative teams.

At least in theory, these articles argue for 'the horizontal corporation' in which people are looking 'outward rather than upward' and where 'managers spend the largest portion of their time looking sideways', to peers and customers. Such a company can 'shed organizational layers' and become 'flatter'. In the horizontal corporation, distinctions among employees as individuals are not as important as the relationships within and among teams.

Ideally, these relationships manifest company values and allow everyone to contribute to the common good, the company's broad vision. Work becomes 'project based rather than position based' as people rotate from project to project. Even managerial responsibility is rotated based on the assumption that most people are capable of being good managers. Managerial responsibility doesn't stick to one person; any one person might be a 'leader on one project, a follower on the next.' 'Titles matter little.'

Directions are not given from the top. Rather, 'coaching' — often among peers — provides the guidance and support necessary for team-based decision-making. The top provides the broad outlines of the vision and values that should guide decision-making.

Information flows quickly and freely across the organization, not just from the top down. Managers are instructed to 'drill into your people a code of conduct where anyone feels free to talk to anyone else in your organization'. This talk can be of the electronic as well as the water cooler type. There is a 'democratization of data' that 'flows where it is needed.'

Thus decentralization is seen as necessary in order to give people the freedom and the permission to create, question, answer and produce. 'Hierarchical systems are obsolete.' They are not flexible enough to allow enough people the freedom they need to innovate and change, to listen and react.

There is remarkable consistency in the direction of these trends over the five-year period covered by the analysis. Among the few differences noted is the absence, in the more recent years, of any mention of 'fun' as a component of the new workplace and new working relationships. 'Having fun' shows up as a positive factor associated with work in the 1991 articles but not in the more recent ones. In light of the current job insecurity due to 'downsizing,' it may be appropriate to emphasize personal growth and empowerment but cloying to imply that the work process can actually be fun.

A second notable difference is an emphasis in 1991 on what MBA schools were doing wrong, especially in their lack of attention to the needs of the new workplace. By 1995, various MBA programs were being highlighted for having changed to include attention to the skills and perspectives that will better prepare managers for the realities indicated by our themes.

These four themes — *values* as the foundation for work; the need to *energize, empower*, and *educate* the work force; the use of *teams* and *collaborations* to drive work processes; and the necessity for *flatter organizational structures* to allow for the first three — appear in *Fortune* magazine as positive trends, necessary for the survival of organizations and the health of the overall economy. It is difficult to estimate the extent to which the trends are reflected in individual workplaces. Many (Lawler, 1992; Sayles, 1993; and O'Toole, 1995) argue that very few businesses have implemented these principles and practices. O'Toole admonishes organizations for irresponsibility in not responding to the need for change which has been apparent for more than a decade. Instead, lip service has been paid to change without real results. Lawler estimates that fewer than 5 per cent of American companies have reformed themselves in line with the themes outlined in *Fortune*. Nonetheless, these themes continue to inform the work of thousands of consultants hired by businesses every year to help make change, and to account for a sizable market in books and teaching materials.

Interest in the themes and uneven attempts at implementing them co-exist with the reality of cutbacks, downsizing, take-overs and other economically driven measures that result in the loss of people's jobs. More than an estimated 3 million jobs were lost in America in 1995; adjusted for inflation, the median wage in 1995 was 3 per cent less than in 1979. Although far more jobs have been added to the economy than lost, nearly two-thirds of downsized workers find only lower paid or temporary jobs, often with reduced or no benefits.[6] Rationales for downsizing that include improving competitiveness in the global economy do not convince critics who cite the absence of a link between excessive CEO compensation and the company's performance,[7] or attribute soaring business profits in the 1990s to stagnant or falling wages rather than greater investment or accelerating productivity.[8] According to Stephen Roach, chief economist for Morgan Stanley Company, the steady economic growth, low inflation and strong profits do not reflect a sustainable rise in productivity — 'they are built on the back of hollowing out labor'.[9] Citing evidence of the 'futility of most downsizing programs', *Money* magazine recommended investment in companies that increase their training budgets in conjunction with any layoffs.[10] Had a majority of US corporations — rather than an estimated 5 per cent — reformed themselves by implementing the themes, the downsizing experience of the 1990s might have been less destructive of individual careers, families and the bonds that maintain community life.

It is unsettling to speak of democratization, humanization and empowerment while at the same time real people are losing their jobs and lives are dramatically disrupted by economic dislocations. But the workplace is indeed changing and the concept of a more empowered, creative workforce co-exists with a workplace that offers less security and more economic uncertainty for the individual worker. People can no longer expect to trade loyalty to and good work for one organization into lifetime employment with that organization. Loyalty and good work must therefore be stimulated for other reasons. Commitment to values and goals — including personal development — that overarch any single organization will need to energize people regardless of the particular source of their current pay check.

Change to new organizational forms, new values and processes is rarely sudden, on an individual, organizational or societal level. As with most major change, there is a lag between new ideas and concepts and their implementation. The process is a non-linear, evolutionary one, with various starting and ending points for different organizations. The same corporations that can be indicted for the absence of social responsibility in the process and outcome of downsizing, can be credited for the introduction of less hierarchy, more listening to employees and customers, and more team-based control over decisions.

There is, understandably, healthy skepticism about the motives of large corporations in introducing flatter structures, team-based management and an emphasis on democratic and humanistic values. Are they doing it in order to create smaller, more profitable structures? Will more than a few ever question the scale of inequality of compensation from CEO to the lowest paid employee?

A critical step in the process of this evolution is education to the ideas of and experiences with new forms of leadership and collaboration throughout the educational process. It is not sufficient — in fact it is counterproductive — to educate students for 12 to 16 years with one model of leadership and work systems and then expect them to adapt to a new system after a few on-the-job workshops.

Rather, what is needed is an influx of people into the labor force, as well as into the community, politics and the family, with a readiness and an expectation for inclusive leadership. An education for leadership and social responsibility will produce people who are comfortable with the concept and practice of inclusive leadership, who will expect it, know how to create it and be eager to participate in it.

Conclusions about Leadership

Several of the *Fortune* articles talk directly about leadership. Significant attention is still paid to individual leaders who are CEOs and presidents. While some of these represent a new, enlightened approach to their organizations, others exhibit qualities associated with traditional, exclusive leadership, such as fear, authoritarianism, ruthlessness and control. One Fortune 500 CEO believes: 'Occasionally it's very important to have a public hanging.'[11] In discussions of how to manage better, an implicit 'great man' (occasionally woman) message still locates leadership in the concentration of power at the top. Therefore, despite the direction of the articles we have examined toward inclusive leadership, leadership is still located in a person, rather than in the process of many people working together.

Our interest is in teasing out of the four themes we have identified the lessons that can be applied to leadership in all sectors of an organization and, by generalization, to non-business organizations as well. Accordingly, leadership that would promote the themes reviewed in *Fortune* includes the following.

1   Ability to conceptualize and articulate the values that underlie and justify the existence of an organization. The leader(s) must behave in ways that demonstrate commitment to the values, both in business decisions and in relationships with others. Leaders must think through the principles of human dignity, respect, social responsibility, democracy, fairness and trust in order to apply and help others apply those principles to the conduct of business.

2   Ability to listen, absorb, interpret and understand the history and culture of the people who give life to an organization. Values derive from and must be tied back to the history of the culture in order to sustain and modify them to guide future behavior. It is not always easy to find the cultural content of an organization, as it often exists in folklore, myths, stories and informal sharing among people. A leader who is not among the

people, who 'doesn't speak their language' will miss the importance of culture to the way people work.

3   Ability to mentor and be mentored. This calls for a re-evaluation of how people — including those in leadership — learn and teach, and for building the expectation of continuous learning into an organization. It is not enough for leaders to function as coaches and mentors; they need to recognize their own need for coaching and allow themselves to be on the receiving end of support as well.

4   Ability to work with others, sometimes in a leaderless team, in order to get the work done. The most important quality of a leader is not having all the answers, but rather creating environments where many people can participate in coming up with answers. These environments promote risk-taking, drive out fear of failure, and encourage questioning. The leader must set the tone for these conditions.

5   Ability to reconceptualize the boundaries among people, job functions and responsibilities, and create new mixtures of human energy. Leaders will encourage interactions among players that may have been unacceptable in the past. Relationships with customers, suppliers and even competitors will not be as controlled (or forbidden) as in the past. Relationships inside the organization will be abundant and guided by the process of work rather than an organizational chart.

6   Ability to obtain and share information broadly. Power can no longer be amassed through control over information. Systems need to be created to get the information where it can be interpreted and used by people.

Education for Leadership and Social Responsibility

What can we derive from this for the design of an education for leadership and social responsibility? In the past, the academy has been justifiably suspicious of the manipulation of curriculum to suit the purposes of business, government or any other non-intellectually driven agenda. Perhaps for the first time, the goals of traditional liberal education and the needs of the modern workplace, as we have just examined them, may be in harmony.

Supporters of traditional liberal education have long enunciated variations on the following outcomes for those who would be liberally educated:

- Individual personal fulfillment
- Development of creativity and a broad vision
- Appreciation for the arts and sensitivity to values
- Appreciation for cultural and historical differences and commonalities
- Tolerance for ambiguity and change
- Civic responsibility
- Ability to analyze and synthesize information
- Proficiency in oral and written communication

This list has been written and rewritten countless times but the basic consistency of the core goals has remained.

In contrast, expectations for how to succeed in business are undergoing enormous change. From the early days of the Industrial Revolution until recently, those expectations rubbed uncomfortably against the more humanistic goals of a liberal education. Traditional business expectations included:

- Preparation for narrow specialization
- Responsiveness to authority
- Fitting in to the organization's culture
- Motivation by individual economic goals
- Individuals as replaceable parts
- Competitive relationships with peers
- Communication controlled through hierarchical relationships

Although these expectations have not disappeared, they are changing. Undoubtedly, the liberal arts list of outcomes would produce an individual better able to exhibit the characteristics of inclusive leadership and active participation than would the list of traditional business expectations.

Our analysis of *Fortune* magazine would lead us to refine the traditional liberal arts list to include the following in an education for leadership and social responsibility.

1 The ability to understand, articulate and apply *values* to individual and group behavior and to make choices within a value context.

2 An appreciation for the components of *culture* and its influence on people and organizations.

3   Interpersonal skills, with a particular emphasis on *listening* and *empathy*.
4   The ability to do *systems thinking* and *common good thinking*.
5   The ability to *problem-find* and *problem-solve*, to *take risks* with innovative approaches, and be *flexible*.
6   The ability to *trust* others, work in *teams*, actively *participate*.
7   The ability to find and use *resources*, including *technological literacy*.

These outcomes are well-served by traditional liberal learning within the context of an institution that models inclusive leadership and social responsibility. We will revisit them in the second half of this book. The reader will note several variations of this list of leadership learning goals/outcomes throughout the book. There is no *one* right way to compose such a list; although the components will be similar, institutional variations will produce different emphases.

The Process of Leadership

The themes we have explored in this chapter are consistent with inclusive leadership. The appropriate language is in place, which is no small step, since people are often stopped in the pursuit of change because of an inability to explain the nature of the change to others. Many in the contemporary business world seem to be using the language of inclusive leadership and social responsibility. But, as noted earlier, few companies are actually implementing it systematically. O'Toole (1995) points out the myriad of factors that impede change and that cause people to resist change, even when it is necessary for survival.

Although the language that describes the principles of a new kind of leadership is in place, there is far less understanding of the processes necessary to operationalize these principles, to put them into place in real organizations. More exploration of and preparation for the process of inclusive leadership is needed. Until now, the education for change and for practicing inclusive leadership was done largely by the corporation, for the corporation. The more wealthy the corporation, the more elaborate the education of employees to understand the principles of inclusive leadership desired by the company. Enlightened businesses without the resources struggle as best they can to help their employees institute work teams, collaborative relationships, and creativity.

The progress of change is limited by reliance on the resources and commitment of each American business firm to educate its employees.

Instead people need to *enter* the work force with the expectations of value-based work, collaborative teams, continuous learning, and less hierarchy — the hallmarks of inclusive leadership — wherever they work, live or play. They need to come prepared to exert leadership when appropriate and to create the conditions to facilitate leadership by those with whom they work.

The next stage in the evolution toward change in leadership styles and processes is educational, beginning in the early grades and becoming more pronounced in higher education's preparation of its graduates. We are not talking about preparing people to be leaders or followers. Rather we are talking about helping people create environments for leadership in all aspects of their life — in their families, communities, governments and work. We need to be preparing people for the process of leadership.

Applications Beyond Work

The same realities that are driving businesses to conceptualize and eventually to implement new forms of leadership and new ways of working together, are driving other institutions as well. Thus many of the same skills and perspectives that will enable individuals to contribute to the workplace will also enable them to participate in ways satisfying to their families and to their changing communities.

Consider the applicability of the characteristics of the twenty-first century workplace we have visited in this chapter to the family, the community, and even to government and other non-profit organizations:

- There is less hierarchy. Less power and control are concentrated in the hands of a few. Who is the boss of the family? How much more democratic are families now than a few generations ago? Are communities trying to include more constituencies in decision-making? Is government streamlining?
- There is more blurring of lines between roles, more cross-functionality, with individuals moving in and out of roles and responsibilities. Who takes out the garbage and changes the cat litter? Who is the bread-winner? Are sex-roles less defining of jobs? Are schools becoming more democratic? Who are the learners?
- Teams are the unit of work rather than the individual. Is there more of an emphasis on consensus, cooperation and collaboration?

- There is more open, two-way communication, a freer flow of information and more emphasis on listening. Human relations experts have long advised family members to listen to one another, to communicate their thoughts and especially their feelings. The technology of the Internet has brought information into the home, the school and the government in a way that has the potential to equalize prior distinctions among people based on access to information.
- People are seen and treated as whole people rather than replaceable parts. There is an attempt to understand and help people meet the needs of their life beyond the office. A holistic approach dominates the primary relationships of the family, is evident in a myriad of new educational approaches, and is necessary for the building and sustaining of communities.
- There is an organizational purpose and responsibility beyond that of unlimited growth and profit-making. Do families encourage and practice social responsibility and value commitment? Do families and communities and the government turn to value-based documents (the Constitution and Bill of Rights), philosophies or religions for guiding principles?
- Opportunities are provided for people to continue learning, creating and developing. Do families and communities and governments believe and practice this with programs for members?
- Focus is on the process of work and leadership rather than on the product after production. If the process is done right, the final product will be good. Is this a child rearing or educational philosophy? Are there parallels with the process of democracy upon which our political system is based?

With some confidence that the themes of inclusive leadership are valid for the contemporary world of work and beyond, we return to the question of implementation. In order to explore further the process of inclusive leadership and how to create environments to facilitate inclusive leadership, we turn in the next chapter to what many may view as a surprising resource — artists.

Notes

1   *Chronicle of Higher Education*, 12 January 1996: A34.
2   *Fortune*, 1 May 1995: 129.

3 *Fortune*, 6 March 1995: 54.
4 *Fortune*, 27 November 1995: 201.
5 *Fortune*, 27 November 1995: 90.
6 *New York Times*, 3 March 1996, pp. 1, 26–29.
7 C.S. Crystal, *New York Times*, 22 February 1996, p. D1.
8 Economic Policy Institute, *Newark Star Ledger*, 3 September 1995, p. 28.
9 *New York Times*, 8 May 1996.
10 *Money*, March, 1996: 11.
11 *Fortune*, 27 November 1995: 90.

Chapter 4

Learning about Leadership from Artists

From the Artists:

> I need feedback from people I trust because you can't hear your own voice, only others can. You can't hear outside in.

> Creativity doesn't just happen. You need to create an environment where people feel free to create along with you.

> There is something dark and scary about getting creative because it is a place of unknowns. You need to have faith and trust in the process, be nonjudgmental and accept a readiness to fail in order to have the courage for creativity.

Why is there a chapter on creativity in a book on education for leadership and social responsibility? Max DePree recognized the connection explicitly in his book *Leadership is an Art* (1989). DePree breaks through the traditional management prescriptions and argues that the expression of human needs, values and experiences are at the core of leadership. Leadership is the manifestation of human relationships.

Artists spend their lives, often with little recognition or monetary reward, exploring and expressing human needs, aspirations, values and experiences. For the most part, artists seek to relate to others by drawing on what they learn through experiences with others and by giving back pieces of their own humanity through the work. Most artists hope their work will touch, inspire and improve the condition of others. This is not unlike the sentiment of fourth grader Kathy, who told us, 'People want to be leaders to make the world good.'

Many have noted the link between what creative people do and what leaders need to do, including problem-find as well as problem-solve; innovate new approaches to familiar situations; visualize change and figure out how to get there (Hutchings, 1986; Vaill, 1989; Richards, 1995).

Beyond this important, obvious overlap of the skill sets and orientations, we believe there are parallels between what creativity *is* and what leadership is. We believe a better understanding of the conditions that facilitate and impede creativity will help us to better understand how to create the conditions that produce a readiness for leadership.

Leadership as Social Process

Both creativity and leadership derive from the interaction of social, cultural and individual variables. Both are located in systems of interaction rather than in particular people. Both need to be understood in the context of the expression of values and judgments.

Csikszentmihalyi (1990) has proposed a systemic perspective on creativity which parallels our understanding of leadership. He maintains that 'the social and cultural conditions, interacting with individual potentialities, (bring) about the objects and behaviors we call "creative".' We believe likewise that social and cultural conditions interact with the potential of individuals to bring about those behaviors we call leadership. Without a better understanding of the *process* of leadership, of the factors that facilitate and impede it, it will be difficult for organizations, despite good intentions, to implement systems that promote inclusive leadership.

For example, among the cultural conditions that influence leadership and creativity are beliefs about where leadership and creativity come from. A traditional definition of leadership, like the traditional definition of creativity, would locate the source in the individual. The qualities for each are believed to be rare, not found in most people, and largely unteachable. In this view, one tends to be 'born talented' or be a 'born leader'. We have heard from the children in Chapter 2, and will hear from the artists later in this chapter, about the importance of early childhood definitions in shaping perceptions of one's own abilities as both a leader and a creative person.

Both leadership and creativity are seen as the basis of great differences between those who have it and those who don't. The children in Chapter 2 portrayed leaders as very different physically from others and often depicted barriers between leaders and the rest of the group. We know that hierarchies are the structural support for maintaining differences and barriers. Likewise, artists are often portrayed as social misfits — eccentric and impractical at best, mentally ill and deviant at worst.

If the above were true, educators would need to pay scant attention to educating for creativity or for leadership. Rather, we would assume that the leaders and the artists would emerge, probably from among the privileged classes and the 'best' schools. Further, society's need for either would be seen as limited. These beliefs are still held by many today (Henry, 1994).

An education for leadership is less about producing leaders and more about producing an understanding of what leadership is so that people have the ability to produce the environments that foster leadership by many. A good leader is one who understands the interaction among the variables that produce leadership and is able to help foster it in others.

The Study

With the recognition, especially during the past decade, that the American workplace needs more innovation and team work to tackle problems of global competition, how to engender more creativity in the workplace has become a vital question. The educational system has been challenged to respond and produce more flexible, creative risk-takers for the American labor force. Though American businesses may have required only a handful of these mavericks and visionaries in the past, the call now — as we saw in Chapter 3 — is for creativity and leadership throughout the organizational structure.

We decided to go right to the source and learn from those who are acknowledged as creative — professional artists. Working with materials and with other people to produce new forms of expression, artists are in a never-ending search for the next innovation. The purpose of our conversations with artists was to derive insights about how they do their work and apply those insights to leadership and the construction of an education for leadership. Through these conversations we hoped to explore our belief that the process of creativity resembles the process of leadership. If we can understand the process of creativity from the point of view of those who create, we may better understand the process of leadership and how to foster it.

During 1992–1995, we interviewed 24 people who make their living as artists. Among the criteria for inclusion in our sample were that the individual is defined by others as an artist, i.e., this was not a hobby or a hidden activity, and the individual participates in demonstrations (shows, exhibitions, performances) for paying audiences or for juries. The range of artistic disciplines includes dancing, acting, directing, painting, sculpting, poetry, writing, music (classical, jazz and rock), weaving and photography. The sample (evenly divided between men and women) represented a range of economic status and ethnic diversity.

The interviews lasted about two hours. Repeatedly the artists told us that the conversations were good experiences for them. Several referred to a therapeutic effect of being able to talk through their own histories and to be challenged to reflect on how they do (and sometimes are unable to do) their work. Much like the children from the earlier chapter, the artists gave us the impression that they were glad somebody was asking them questions and listening to their answers.

Key Findings

The Creative Process

Artists consciously focus on the process of creating (or problem-finding and solving), not on the final product.
There is great faith in the process of creativity, that it will yield results, and that the artist's task is to engage in the process with his or her whole, authentic self. Clearly, cynicism and mistrust, sentiments that are often expressed in creative art, do not characterize the artist's approach to the process of being creative and producing.

The process is described as a series of encounters of the person with others, with the self, the environment, and with materials and ideas.
The process is a series of working relationships that clarify, amend, and help shape a product. The others in the relationship may be colleagues, artists living and dead, works of art, or any other people and ideas to which the artist has access through books, art or personal experience.

The creative process is in part a communication process between the artist and the materials of his or her discipline.
The communication is two-way, so the artist is listening to the materials — the notes, the colors, the ideas — as well as speaking to them.

The process itself is often an exciting human relationship which many artists characterize as a 'high' and as having a satisfying physical as well as emotional effect.
In the words of the artists: 'you never know where you're going'; 'you don't know where it will end, you only know it feels right while you are doing it'. It is in many cases described as so 'intoxicating' or 'addictive' that even though the work may be draining, frustrating and endless, the process of working is exciting.

Artists are guided in the process of creativity by basic principles and beliefs about themselves and the value of the process.

Even though 'you don't know where you are going in advance of getting there', the artists know that they have 'something to say'. That 'something' is pushing to get out, to find expression. Though they may not know what the final product will look like, they are guided by a faith and confidence that if they work at their discipline, problem-finding and solving, the right things will emerge. The artists value and honor the process because of what it has yielded for them and for others in the past and they trust it will be successful in the future.

All of the artists value the role of collaboration in their work. While some use it more than others, nearly all wish they could do more.

Most of the artists have worked collaboratively to build a product. Although collaborations may not represent the bulk of their work, they seem to be particularly fruitful, stimulating experiences. The need to orient one's art to the expressions of another calls on a dimension of communication that the artists describe with great joy.

All of the artists value feedback from other artists, most during the process of creation. Several have on-going relationships with mentors and many are themselves teachers. They all feel part of a community of artists and several have taken active roles in organizing local artists to supply each other with a living community.

Regular engagement in the creative process is critical.

The artists agree that they must work every day on the art. They feel guilty, anxious and depressed if they don't. Even if only a few minutes a day can be devoted to it, 'you need to keep wrestling with the ideas and problems'. Many note the necessity to 'be ready' for the as yet unknown time when all the practicing and experimenting come together in 'a magical moment' of production. It is continuous engage-ment in the process of creativity that readies one for production.

Most artists work on several projects simultaneously.

Many switch mediums, from painting to sculpture; from compos-ing music to composing poetry. Most have projects that they will put away and get back to at a later time, sometimes many years later. These unfinished projects constitute future agendas for many of the artists. And indeed we saw the results of projects that were left uncompleted for years and then finished in a week. The projects that are incubating simultaneously influence each other and become part of each other's creative process.

The artists note that having multiple projects underway provides a means of stress reduction, as it provides alternative process streams for the artist to enter when temporarily blocked by any one.

Identity

All had their identity as an artist formed early in life by positive rein-forcement and acknowledgment from significant people, usually parents and teachers.

Though some had negative experiences with a teacher early on, with the support of adults the vast majority learned to value their own ideas, impulses and energy. 'I learned that what I have to say is worth giving out to others.' 'People liked what I did, so I did more.' Most were also guided to appreciate the importance of learning more from others. Most 'took lessons', though often in a discipline other than the one in which they wound up.

Most had parents who valued the arts and many have memories of their parents performing or just enjoying some art form. The world of the arts was not a strange or mysterious place to them as children. There was a feeling of access to the arts to which the child could relate and make a contribution.

Many were told that they were talented or had a gift, although now most believe almost everyone can draw, sing, compose, dance, etc., given the right opportunity and support.

Many felt lonely or isolated in their pursuit of creativity in childhood and not until later, when they found a community of people all pur-suing the same artistic endeavor, did they feel really comfortable with the identity of artist.

This often happened in a graduate or professional school setting or with a first job in the arts. Most reported the importance of sustaining a sense of membership in a community of artists in their adult lives and all were successful in doing so.

Although they received support for the artistic pursuits, most also report receiving mixed messages about the desirability of becoming an artist.

Many picked up a judgment from teachers that people can't be both smart and creative. Others were troubled by the impracticality of being an artist because of its limited economic return.

The women artists reveal more self-doubt and doubt about the worth of their art.

As girls, many of the women received the message that while they were good at their art, they would never excel in their field. Many of the women artists still feel a conflict between the demands of their art and their desire to have a family and do other things. They are more afraid than men of being consumed by the creative process to the detriment of their families.

Facilitative Conditions

There are some specific physical and psychological conditions that help facilitate the creative process.

Among the conditions mentioned repeatedly by the artists are:

1   *Uninterrupted time.*   The length of time is less important than the certainty of no external demands. Generally the more time the better, although several artists break long periods into shorter spurts of actual work time.

2   *Materials and supplies and a comfortable physical place in which to work.*   There is a need for ready access to the materials of one's discipline — in abundance and at hand. Materials both inspire and facilitate creativity. A scarcity of materials or the fear of running out of materials is a serious limitation on even entering into the creative process. There are obvious monetary implications to this necessity, especially for those whose disciplines rely on expensive technologies. The need for a comfortable, familiar, work space dedicated only to the artist's work . . . 'a place where I can let go of the mundane . . .' was equally important.

3   *Quiet.*   The artists consistently speak of the need for quiet within their work space. They do not mean silence, since they often introduce noises, especially music, into the environment. They mean noise that they define as distracting, i.e., people in the household talking, music that is not of their choosing, the phone ringing and the answering machine responding, etc. Artists speak of the need to listen to themselves, to the voice that is directing the creativity. The necessary intensity of listening requires focus that can be distracted by outside interferences.

4   *External deadlines for work.*   Although the demands of the market can also be experienced as an obstacle to creativity,

most of the artists cited a deadline for an upcoming public obligation as a motivator for their work. A schedule of perform-ances, concerts, exhibits or other contracts for work put some time pressure on the creative process and often help propel the work.

5   *No close scrutiny of the creative process by others.* The artists need to set their own parameters for work and to have only the final product scrutinized. They are the best judges of how to organize and conduct the process itself.

There is a state of mind that artists associate with their creativity and there are techniques to get to that mental state.

The techniques mentioned include meditation; exercise, from slow walking to intense aerobic activity; listening to music; and free writing. The latter involves spontaneously putting on paper whatever is on one's mind without regard to organization and then discarding what has been written.

The right state of mind is non-cognitive and not cerebral, but thrives on an energy that comes from another place.

One of the biggest challenges for artists is to 'lighten up on the emphasis on analytical thinking' and 'don't be so mental'. Many spoke of a source of creative energy that is simultaneously relaxed, open, trusting and excited. In their best creative moments they are not think-ing in the traditional sense. 'Academic knowledge and analysis work against creativity'. The challenge is to 'get totally in the moment and let the energy come out', to 'let go of the fear' and just do.

The artists note that they can't do other kinds of work during the creative process. Such necessary tasks and concerns as bookkeeping, filing, any kind of organizing, emotional problem-solving and house-hold management issues get in the way. They seem to 'call on another part of the brain' that cannot operate simultaneously with creativity.

There is some fear associated with entering the creative process.

It is a 'dark and scary place' because it is not predictable and the artist has to be self-revealing. The creative process is by definition ambiguous and often lonely. There is always uncertainty about the final outcome and about the judgments that will be made. The artists recog-nize their own vulnerability at the hands of the process but their trust in the benefits of the process, as well as support from others, and the highs they get from self-expression and sharing, keep encouraging them into the dark and scary places.

The artists are wary of predictability and things that come easily.

They do not want to repeat successes but rather move on to something unknown. They need a problem to work with and fear becoming comfortable and getting 'caught up in just one thing'. They also fear 'destructive perfectionism' which not only results in constant unhappiness but in never being able to let go of a final product and let it have a life of its own.

Self-doubt is the killer of creativity. The creative state of mind is non-judgmental, allows room for failure, and trusts in the self and the process of creativity.

This condition then allows the artist to follow his or her instincts and impulses with no concern for achieving a prescribed outcome but with only the goal of interacting with the materials and with one's ideas, and often being surprised by the outcome. According to one artist, 'I need to make a lot of stupid mistakes.' And another, 'I need to learn from the accidents.'

Blocks to work are common and become both expectable and acceptable. The block is overcome by faith and confidence in the self and in the process of creative work.

The artists were not stopped by blocks or an inability to work. Many of them had found ways to redefine block to see it as a natural part of the creative process and to give themselves permission to experience it. Some see it as a change element, a step on the way to the next creative activity. Some define it as 'part of the balance of the process'.

Past experience, the experiences of others, and the support of sympathetic others allow the artist to believe that the block is temporary, that they will be able to work again in a short period of time. There is great faith and trust that the creative process will yield as yet unforeseen results.

Ideas for creative work abound. The challenge is actualizing the ideas through the creative process.

Artists from all disciplines reveal that they have an abundance of ideas, most of which do not materialize into products. 'I'm never at a loss for ideas'; 'I get 1000 ideas a day'; 'there is a constant idea stream going through my mind'; 'there is so much to express'; 'inspiration is everywhere.'

Sources include the raw materials of the discipline which often suggest possibilities to the artist; memories and experiences of daily living which suggest patterns or metaphors; the art of others; self-reflection on one's own reactions and emotions and understandings.

There is a need to have one's work recognized by others.

For most of the artists, the creative process does not stop with the production of a work of art. Rather, it is not complete until the work is shared with others, with an audience. Very few of the artists could imagine themselves without an audience for their work, since 'giving it to others is what it's all about'. 'It would be selfish to do it without the audience'. Many spoke of the final goal of the creative process as the ability to invite others in to share your work and on rare, but extremely important occasions, to transform or transport the audience with the work.

Not only is the audience 'part of the fun' and 'mildly addictive', it is also part of the relationship that fires the creative process. Most spoke of a communication process with the audience. The audience is 'a very important source of energy' for the artist.

There is recognition of the need for authenticity with the audience who will receive the work. 'The more at ease and unselfconscious the artist, the more the audience will be drawn in.' Most artists have faith in audiences — that they will sense the validity and integrity of a piece of work that has been produced through a process of creation that was open and honest.

Implications for Leadership

How do these insights provided by creative artists help us better understand leadership? We believe that the similarities between the human capacity for leadership and the human capacity for creativity are compelling. The parallels proceed from the following assumptions:

- the capacity for leadership and the capacity for creativity are present in most human beings, of all ages;
- leadership and creativity are elicited by environmental, social and cultural factors;
- self-awareness and an awareness of others are at the foundation of both.

Artists teach us the following principles about leadership which can be used to guide both designated leaders — managers, parents, teachers, politicians or CEOs — and those with whom they work.

1   Focus on the process of finding and solving problems, not on the as yet unknown outcome. Do not presume the outcome;

let it happen by working with your raw materials. The raw materials are other people and technologies, and the information and ideas they generate. As with artists, leaders need to listen to their raw materials and get the most out of them. Again, don't presume limitations, but once determined, work within the given human parameters.

2   Do not assume a linear flow of work on a single project. Rather, let several work projects proceed simultaneously and derive a positive influence from each other. Let people work on more than one project at once in several, possibly overlapping work teams. Make sure information about various projects is shared widely so implications and applications may be drawn.

3   The artists tell us that the process of creativity is a series of encounters with others, with the self, the environment, and with materials and ideas. The same is true for leadership. The process for both is a series of working relationships, information gathering, listening and empathizing, imagining, planning and executing. The leadership process at its best can be exciting and exhilarating, in part because it involves the movement of ideas and people in a process of creation. The creativity of the leader is measured by the ideas and energy of the people in the group. The new ideas that emerge are a result of good leadership that allows people to define their common purpose and take responsibility for improvements. It is an exciting process that will itself give rise to more leadership within the group. Like a jazz ensemble, when the leadership process is really working leadership will be at once everywhere and difficult to detect.

4   The artists affirm the role of values and principles in guiding their work. As we heard from the business community, values are at the foundation of successful organizations and successful leadership. But it is not enough to say so. The values must be operationalized and shared in order to serve as a touchstone for decisions. There is deep confidence in the value and ultimate productivity of the process of creativity that can be paralleled in the process of leadership. If inclusive values are guiding the process, there may be murkiness about the eventual outcome but there should be certainty that the process is right — inclusive, democratic, respectful and aimed toward the common good. This faith in the process, which ultimately is faith in people and guiding values, allows leaders to continue in spite of obstacles and an uncertain outcome.

5   The role of collaboration, support and feedback is as important in the emergence of leadership as it is in the emergence of creativity. The artist and the leader rely on interactions with others to inspire, refine and validate their behavior. In turn, they learn how to support and encourage others. Thus good leaders are also good supporters of other leaders. Support does not imply consensus, but rather participation, encouragement, assistance and opportunity.

6   Continuous engagement in the process of leadership — as leader, as follower, as mentor or mentee — readies people to jump in and out of leadership roles as necessary. Engagement with others in the process is rehearsal for unknown opportunities. People become comfortable with the process of leadership and derive enjoyment out of engaging in the role of leader as well as helping others with leadership roles. Leadership needs to be cultivated and demystified early in life. More children need adult encouragement to pursue behaviors consistent with inclusive leadership. We have heard from the children in Chapter 2 about the importance of early encouragement to form an identity consistent with *leader*. This is not unlike the reports of artists who nearly consistently received early support for their interest in creativity.

7   It is important for children and adults to recognize that leadership is not a weird or rare human trait. There are many others who value and engage in inclusive leadership behaviors. An interest in problem-solving, working with others toward common goals, envisioning those goals, and encouraging others, are ingredients of leadership that are valuable and cultivatable in most people. Leadership, like creativity, knows no gender, racial, social class or age boundaries. Any preconceived ideas about the association of these qualities with social categories is a social construction that feeds bias, limits opportunities, and deprives all of us.

8   The same conditions that help the artist produce also help workers in teams, including leaders, produce. Leadership, like creativity, can be facilitated by:
   - *Time* dedicated to thinking, listening, brainstorming, and working at problems
   - *Access* to materials and supplies, including *all the constituencies* the leadership touches. The access needs to be abundant and immediate, not mediated by others.

- *External demands* for product
- *Autonomy,* absence of close scrutiny

9 The artists' suggestions for 'getting to the right state of mind' are applicable to cultivating leadership. They include introspection and sensitivity to the environment; having time to reflect; letting go of fear and too much focus on the cerebral; and becoming totally involved in the process of leading and sharing with others. The fear of creativity being a 'dark and scary place' resonates with the children's perceptions that leadership is scary and lonely. This perception may have more to do with entering the process of leadership in which one becomes very vulnerable to others, one's values and sensibilities are exposed, the future is ambiguous, and one becomes dependent on the responsiveness and acceptance of others in order to be validated and continue. The processes of creativity and leadership are similar in their potential to totally capture the participants as well as in their potential for exhilaration and great discovery. Both the artist and the leader persevere because of a faith that the process will produce results and be worth the risks. Leaders, like artists, are pushing the boundaries of the known and the taken-for-granted. They are not content with yesterday's successes but look for new and different approaches to bring out the best.

10 Leaders need to learn the importance of reserving hasty judgments about themselves and others in order to make risk-taking possible. According to the artists, fear of failure and self-doubt kill creativity, and, according to the children, they also obliterate leadership before it begins.

Implications for Educating for Leadership and Social Responsibility

There is much to be learned about leadership from engagement in the process of creativity. We need to assure that there are ample opportunities, within the context of diverse subject matters, for students to use a creative process. Exposure to the arts and to artists is also an important ingredient in the development of inclusive leadership. The lessons derived from an understanding of the process of creativity, from one's own and the experiences of others, are generalizable to the process of leadership. Most prominent are the abilities to:

- Access resources and be open to the possibilities presented by the raw materials at hand. What are the resources available? Are some being overlooked because of old assumptions about their characteristics? Can familiar resources be put to new, re-combined uses? Creativity and leadership will both be served by enhancing the skills associated with the acquisition of information. These include the skills of listening, of discovering patterns, of seeing systems of interconnected parts, of questioning the taken-for-granted and other critical inquiry and communication skills, including proficiency with information technologies.

- Develop faith in a process based on values and overcome blocks and frustrations; What are the values that guide this process of exploration, discovery or collaboration? Why are these values important and likely to lead to a positive outcome? The ability to recognize, articulate and analyze values that guide our behaviors — whether we are weaving a basket, managing a corporation or parenting a teenager — puts us in touch with our humanity and makes difficult decisions clearer.

- Appreciate the role of collaboration in the processes of creativity and leadership. How can ideas and products be improved by entering into the process in collaboration? What are the values that sustain a collaborative relationship? Paradoxically, creativity is the process that can actualize what is a 'unique pattern of potentialities' (Kneller, 1965) in individuals but, as we have heard from the artists, creativity relies on some form of human collaboration, if only with an audience or with the ideas of others. At its best, collaboration heightens the 'unique pattern of potentialities' by positioning them in relationship to the patterns of other individuals for an infinite number of potentialities. It is only with repeated experiences with diverse collaborations that both the process and the values that support it become trusted. For inclusive leadership, trust in the process of collaboration, which ultimately rests on trust in self and others, is essential.

- Students should be given positive feedback about their own creativity early and often. We also need to give space for failure. According to Robert Schank (1988:61), 'Schools have had their greatest effect on squelching American innovation by instilling in so many of us a great fear of failure.' The process of creativity and the lives of great artists need to be demystified and discussed openly in order to make creativity accessible to ordinary people. The role of hard work, perseverance, support, risk-taking, courage, confidence and interaction with others needs to be emphasized. With an understanding of the conditions that encourage creativity, students should have the opportunity and the expectation to encourage the creativity of others.

The principles of inclusive leadership with which we began in Chapter 1 have been illuminated by the ideas of children, the business community and artists. All three groups have attested to the need to shift to this model in order to elicit the best from people, keep them learning and growing, and to have the most people possible participating in shaping solutions to the challenges of the twenty-first century. All three groups value quality and recognize that it can be best attained through non-authoritarian, participatory systems. The values that are implicit in all three support human dignity and mutual respect, freedom from fear, opportunity to participate, and freedom of expression. Although they may appear to have little in common, children, the business community and artists have in fact revealed a sense of a common good that unites them.

With this encouragement, we turn to the practical question of how to educate so that people enter their jobs and communities with the expectation that these values will prevail and with a readiness to help foster the inclusive leadership that the values require.

Part Two

Applications: Building Educational Communities for Leadership and Social Responsibility

Chapter 5

Planning and Implementing an Education for Leadership and Social Responsibility

From college faculty and staff:

> I spend all of my time trying to keep up with the demands of my students and my research. How do you expect me to get involved in changing the way things are done around here? That's not my job.

> The more things change, the more they stay the same.

> Let's stop planning and start doing.

> You're putting the inmates in charge of the asylum.

Planning for change should not be looked on as preliminary to the real work. It is as much a part of the real work of change as the actual programs, new organizations and revised curriculums that will follow. How we plan for and implement change provides critical opportunities to clarify and model the principles of inclusive leadership and social responsibility. In the academy, planning is usually defined as a necessary, laborious process that is part of somebody else's job, the results of which are passed on to administrators and faculty to implement. This top-down planning is antithetical to inclusive leadership. It deprives organizations of the best thinking and alienates participants who, because they weren't involved in planning for change, cannot effectively implement change.

In the past decade, the 'quality' movement has inspired application of Total Quality Management to higher education, with a resulting focus on students, teamwork and continuous improvement of the processes of education (Deming, 1986; Audette, 1990; Cornesky et al., 1991; Seymour, 1992; Wolverton, 1994). The quality movement has helped to involve more people in the process of planning and to appreciate the role of brainstorming and risk-taking. It is hoped that educators can reclaim the right and responsibility to help plan the directions our institutions will take, and steer a course between autocratic governance and a process that makes an institution 'incapable of . . . an expedited decision' (Zemsky and Massy, 1995). Those directions have a profound effect on the lives of the individuals who are participants in the institution.

The Processes of Planning and Learning

In an educational environment, almost everyone thinks he or she knows something about learning. That is the business we are in. Few, however, profess to be expert planners. In many institutions, this job is outsourced to specialists or is institutionalized in an Office of Planning, whose personnel do not generally interact with most faculty and students. Higher education has created a specialty out of a basic organizational process that can be successful only if many people understand it and get involved. This involvement can be made easier by the acknowledgment that educators really do know more about planning than they or others may think, by virtue of their knowledge of the learning process. Because there is considerable similarity between the processes of learning and planning, our familiarity with learning can be used to facilitate successful planning.

In the framework of inclusive leadership, when we speak of learning we are speaking of *interactive* learning that relies on the active engagement of the learner with others in an open and supportive environment. Likewise, planning must be collaborative, interactive and ongoing. The processes are similar in at least the following ways:

- Both are *change oriented* with the goal of improvement. Both need to appreciate the developmental nature of change, while allowing for the occasional 'ah ha' breakthrough moments of insight. Change is generally incremental for both individuals and institutions and is made easier by self awareness, including knowledge of one's history.
- Both processes are *influenced by* a context of values, relationships among people and access to resources. Key questions for both individual and institutional growth are: How much support is there for risk-taking, failure, achievement, feedback and creativity? How much shared responsibility is there for the outcome of learning or planning? Whose responsibility are those students who do not learn or those plans that are not implemented?

- Both processes must acknowledge the *necessity of systems thinking* for accurate understanding, constructive feedback and goal-setting. Only a holistic approach that takes the whole person or the entire institution into account will produce good results.
- For both learning and planning, *active involvement* of people in the process increases the likelihood of the success of the process. Involvement in one's own learning or in institutional planning increases understanding of and commitment to the goals and engenders creativity.
- Characteristics that make for successful planning and implementation — honesty, openness, consultation, interactive communication (especially listening), assessment, feedback, facts, continuity and decentralization — are also those that provide the best context for learning.

Others have recognized the links between planning and learning. Michael (1973) maintains that learning should be the most important product of strategic planning and Senge (1990) proposes that healthy organizations in the twenty-first century will be learning organizations for themselves and for all of their stakeholders. These writers — and organizations that are implementing new ideas — do not recommend adoption of traditional elements of the learning process, such as rigid classroom structure and order (assigned seats, ringing bells), hierarchy (teacher as authority) and competition (for grades and attention). Rather, increasing value is being given in the workplace and in the process of planning to spontaneity and creativity, teamwork, collaboration and decentralization. The same elements that produce successful learning produce successful planning.

Characteristics of an Inclusive Planning Process

While each institution must design its own plan according to its own distinctive vision, the components and methods of planning and implementing change should include several similarities that reflect our discussion of inclusive leadership.

- *Process values.* Planning is guided by values as well as procedures and timetables, and people should be aware of the values that support the processes of planning and implementation at their institution. Consistent with the principles of inclusive leadership, process values will be rooted in democratic participation, respect and belief in the efficacy of people and groups. Articulation of these values by the participants, early in the process of planning, will help establish them as the foundation for the education that is being constructed. It should be made clear that the processes themselves — the way people go about planning and implementing — and not just the outcomes, are important to the institution. At no time are ignoble means justified by noble ends; the means must therefore conform to the implicit ends — the values of inclusive leadership.

- *Systems thinking.* Use of a whole-system approach to planning and implementation. Planning for the improvement of student learning and the attainment of the vision of the student graduate prepared for inclusive leadership in the twenty-first century must involve and enrich all of the participants in the organization — the faculty, staff, community (including families, businesses and non-profits), alumni, board members and administrators.

- *Cross-boundary working.* Diminished emphasis on traditional boundaries among divisions, departments, units and statuses of individuals when organizing to get the planning work done and the changes implemented. People should be organized across traditional boundaries into work groups, study teams, implementation and evaluation committees. The participation of constituencies outside the immediate campus should also be encouraged. 'Planning conversations' often lead to new working relationships that will prove valuable for other purposes for individuals as well as the institution.

- *Collaboration, consultation, and feedback.* These methods will need to be discussed at an early stage of the planning process, beginning with involvement in organizing the planning process itself. Ways to accomplish them include the use of email, networked discussions, focus groups, surveys and conversations. No method is more effective than representative working groups and the relationships that develop within them. A systems approach will assure that each working group represents all the diverse voices that need to be heard.

All members of the college community need to understand that while they are invited into the planning process, not to participate is an abdication of membership responsibilities that harms the organization and contradicts the principles of inclusive leadership. Visions for what the institution can accomplish can come from sources located anywhere within the institution, and the planning process needs to assure that all voices are heard. This message needs to be conveyed — through whatever means are available — within all organizational arenas of the campus, at local as well as public occasions, by the president, by senior administrators and faculty, by staff, union and student leaders. Planning is not *more* work (although it is necessary to be sympathetic to this initial, understandable reaction), it is *the* work.

Recognizing the Need for Change

The need for change — specifically change toward a more integrated education that focuses on preparation for inclusive leadership — must be widely acknowledged. Getting people to feel that change is necessary, especially change that will involve them in new work and new ways of thinking and doing, is often met with firm resistance (O'Toole, 1995). Understandably, it is more difficult to engage those who feel comfortable with their present circumstances and those who believe they have something to lose if things change than it is to engage those who feel dissatisfied, frustrated and disappointed with the current ways of doing things.

The first step toward change, therefore, involves coming to grips with those conditions in education that are distressing, depressing and enervating — conditions that are abundantly reported in the national and professional media as well as in the experience of our classrooms and professional lives. The confrontation with dissatisfactions needs to be taken out of hallways and cafeterias, out of self or other blame, out of 'we–they' analyses and elevated to public discussion within the educational community of the campus. Here is a good opportunity to involve the larger community, especially K–12 educators, parents and students, with the campus community in these conversations. New alliances can be forged by bringing together several groups composed of mixed campus and community constituencies to address the question 'What's wrong with education today, specific to our town and campus?'

We would expect that an inventory of educational concerns, constructed by faculty, staff, students, alumni, and administrators, will include most of the following interrelated issues:

- Public misperceptions and lack of public confidence in education and educators. Many items fall into this category, all having to do with accountability. Included here are questions about faculty workloads and the accusation that faculty don't teach enough, that they and their institutions care only about grant-funded research, not about teaching and learning. Can we measure the value that is added by a four-year degree? Do educators know what the most important outcomes are and how to achieve them?

- Self-criticism by educators. We educators are not being true to our mission. The rhetoric of curriculum plans, catalog promises, and public statements conflicts with what we actually deliver. We're not sure what we actually deliver.
- Concerns about declining enrollments, low rates of retention and graduation rates. In addition to the impact of lost tuition revenues on the budget, low enrollments and high attrition are interpreted as reflecting the poor quality of the institution. In a few cases the concern may be for 'over-enrollment' and the question of selectivity, given limited resources available to support a large population.
- Complaints about the lack of preparedness of incoming students at every level, including kindergarten. The students are defined as not 'ready to learn' because they lack the skills, talent and/or motivation. The prior education they have received, mass media, and the home environment are blamed for these deficiencies.
- Faculty burnout and morale issues. Many faculty do not feel appreciated, respected or intellectually alive, and are not proud of their association with their institution. The culprits here range from 'the public' to students to administrators to colleagues. In a recent international survey, 58 per cent of US faculty said their administrations were 'often autocratic' (England 64 per cent; Australia 63 per cent). Fifty-seven per cent said relationships between faculty and administration were fair or poor (Australia 69 per cent). Sixty-four per cent said they were personally 'not at all influential' in shaping their institution's academic policy (England 74 per cent; Australia 75 per cent) (Altbach and Lewis, 1995).
- The educational environment is not what it should be. The lack of a supportive intellectual and emotional community is manifested in the pervasiveness of turf wars and destructive politics. The environment discourages risk-taking and experimenting by faculty, administrators or students. At the US Naval Academy, a 'culture of hypocrisy prevails', according to a faculty member's critique (Barry, 1996).

- Finances. Concerns range from low salaries and inadequate resources to cutbacks in government and private support to running the institution with a deficit operating budget.

Going through this exercise will not be as depressing as it may seem. A liberation and sense of community can come from sharing individual frustrations and acknowledging that the frustrations are widespread. The process itself can be an antidote for malaise as people get involved, talk and listen, express feelings and fears and ultimately renew hope for improvement. This should be done in small groups, within general areas (i.e., faculty, staff, students, parents, administrators), using brainstorming techniques. The results can then be processed and distributed to everyone to show commonality as well as differences.

The danger of the exercise is that it may result in 'person or culture blaming' rather than in a commitment to change. To avoid this possibility, a large group follow-up session could introduce the national and global context in which local complaints reside. A commitment to change will derive from the belief that the situation, though serious, is far from hopeless. Reference might also be made to the numerous examples of success with whole-system change that individual schools or school districts are having around the country (Jervis and Montag, 1991; Sizer, 1992). The point of these discussions is to confirm that the dissatisfactions of individual institutions are shared nationally and globally and that individual institutions are trying creative new approaches to meet the challenges.

Linking the Future to the Past

Once the need for change and the belief that improvement is possible are established, it is possible to sketch a vision of alternative futures. The first step to envisioning institutional future is having knowledge of institutional past on which to build. In the work of planning it is essential to link proposed change to the historical purposes, goals and values of the institution.

Most institutions have formulated statements of purpose or mission, found in college catalogues, student handbooks, the institutional strategic plan and other official publications. Key documents which mark significant moments in an institution's development are often accompanied by presidential addresses and other statements of institutional purpose and goals. Sometimes these are memorialized in slogans on plaques on buildings or under photographs of past presidents. Whether their content was lived in the institution or not, these statements are worth summarizing as a way of reminding the community of the noble purposes for which the institution was founded, the evolving identity of the institution, and the role of change in bringing the institution to its current state. The constituencies will come to know and cherish the institution more to the extent that they feel part of an organizational life with a history and a future.

The goal is to remind participants, and indeed to insure that the process of change is organic, consistent with, and honors the history of the institution, its constituencies and its culture (Neuman, 1993). Change agents need to demonstrate that although the content of the changes eventually proposed may be dramatic and bold, the processes of planning and implementing change have a tradition consistent with the historical, stated values of the institution.

Because the initiative to educate for leadership and social responsibility (ELSR) is central to the identity and the future of the institution, it must fit comfortably into the institutional strategic plan. The rationale and projected outcomes of the plans for ELSR should be reflected in the strategic plan of the institution. There it should be made clear that the commitment to educate for leadership and social responsibility is an institutional commitment, supported by the president and the governing board. Public statements to that effect should be made and widely disseminated.

ELSR planning needs to take into account many variables that are or will be important to a particular institution. Strategic planning at the macro-level will assist the planning for an education for leadership and social responsibility by providing strategic information important to the future of the institution — demographic projections, resource analysis, local and national political developments, etc. In turn the philosophy and goals of an education for inclusive leadership will influence how the institution defines itself for the twenty-first century in its strategic planning.

Sugar Plums

While clarity of historical and contemporary purpose is essential, it is not sufficient. The next step is to move beyond institutional purpose to vision. Peter Senge (1990) reminds us that 'Purpose is similar to direction, a general heading. Vision is a specific destination, a picture of a desired future.' In spite of jokes and criticisms of 'the vision thing', it is actually a lot more concrete than 'the purpose thing' with which most of us are more familiar. Its concreteness, however, makes vision more demanding of analysis and accountability. Vision relies for its integrity on the values that underlie the stated purpose. We are not talking about visions that 'dance in your head'. In effective visioning, the sugar plums are defined as to size and shape and, most importantly, goals and strategies are set for their attainment.

From general statements of purpose — what we do and why we exist —we move to specific questions of why we do it and how we can do it better. The latter call for the articulation of values and vision. Despite great variation in specific purpose, all educational institutions share the fundamental purpose of teaching and learning. Visions must therefore focus on the learners and their teachers, however broadly defined. Importantly, it should not be expected that visions will spring only from the head of the president. They often evolve from the planning conversations among those who are in close contact with students. Visions need to be clearly articulated and embraced by key administrators. Jealousy about 'who said it first' often undermines an institution's ability to articulate the vision. Such ownership struggles signal that more fundamental work needs to be done on the commitment to the common good and the belief that individual success is tied into institutional success at all levels. One person or group of people do not own the spirit and vision of an institution. It is by definition a collective product. Various individuals and departments may contribute particular perspectives, words and projects, but these make sense only within the larger context of contributing to an education for leadership and social responsibility — which is ultimately measured in the lives of graduates.

The only place to start a vision for change is with the students who are the purpose for our institutional existence. We need to move from that recognition to a vision of the outcome of the education we are providing for the student. Even when planning for institutional fund raising, physical plant development, faculty development, budget allocation, structural organization and the myriad of other on-going institutional concerns, the vision of the graduate should influence planning. The vision must be focused on educational outcomes and on providing the environment to produce them. While each campus will come to its own conclusions, our explorations in the preceding chapters result in the following statement of leadership learning goals, a somewhat enhanced version of the inventory constructed in Chapter 3.

1 The ability to understand, articulate and apply *values* to individual and group behavior and to make decisions within a value context.

2 An appreciation for the components of *diverse cultures* and their influence on people and organizations.

3 *Interpersonal skills*, with a particular emphasis on *listening* and *empathy*.

4 The ability to do *systems thinking* and *common good thinking*, with the resulting *tolerance for ambiguity* and understanding of limits.

5 The ability to *problem-find, problem-solve, take risks* with innovative approaches, and be *flexible*.

6 The ability to *trust* others, *collaborate* in and lead *teams*, and work effectively in *horizontal* organizations.

7 The ability to *manage* and *reduce conflict*.

8 The ability to find and use *resources*, including *technological literacy*.

In its sharpest focus the vision is not directly concentrated on the institution (its survival, reputation, market position). Rather, it illuminates the product — the graduating student preparing for problem-finding and solving and socially responsible leadership in the twenty-first century. The student is both the recipient and the embodiment of the vision. The transformative power of the vision is that its achievement is dependent on the environment created by the faculty, other students, community, administration, staff, alumni and governing bodies. They will be held accountable for working together to model collaboration, systems thinking, democratic values and respect for one another. Thus, achieving the vision of the graduating student prepared for inclusive leadership and social responsibility has a powerful impact on everyone associated with the institution.

Organizing to Plan and Implement Change

In organizing to actualize a vision that is focused on student learning, the entire institution must become consciously knowledgeable and supportive of the leadership learning goals and the teaching–learning process, in and out of the classroom. All campus community members will feel more valued to the extent that they believe they share a common purpose and vision — providing the environment to educate students for inclusive leadership. The engagement of the whole campus in a common vision, using common language and values that are reflected in activities and daily behavior, goes a long way toward helping people redefine their own importance to the mission of the college. The activity of planning and implementing change serves as an integrative mechanism for divisions and departments that may be operating as discrete units with separate responsibilities. The framework of inclusive leadership helps to blur traditional boundaries between defined units and pushes the whole system to respond to the student and to associates as leaders and responsible participants.

In the language of the Total Quality Movement (Deming, 1986; Seymour, 1992; Wolverton, 1994): Primarily, the focus is on the student as customer and on the collaborative efforts to help the customer succeed (learn). Secondarily, all members of the college community are each other's customers. Given the aversion of some to using the word *customer* in academe, it should be emphasized that this *service to the customer* ethic goes beyond accommodation, courtesy, honesty and efficiency, as important as these qualities are. Ultimately, customer satisfaction rests on the success of the student as a learner. This calls for a shift in role definitions for teachers from dispensers of wisdom to en-ablers, mentors and collaborators (we will have more to say about this in Chapter 6), a shift for students from passive receivers and regurgitators of information to active shapers and users of opportunities to interact with people and ideas (Chapter 7), and for others from administrative and service personnel to active, caring role models who are themselves challenged to learn.

Preliminary to organizing, two questions need to be addressed. The first is 'What kind of leadership is necessary for the twenty-first century?' All campus constituencies should be asked to contribute to this question's answer, which can then be formulated into a community response by an elected steering committee for planning. The second question — 'Should our college/university be preparing students to participate in this kind of leadership as both leaders and followers?' — requires a linking of the ingredients of inclusive leadership to the mission of the institution to legitimize the focus on leadership and social responsibility (or whatever words are used to express the values of inclusive leadership) as an overarching institutional concern. Although we believe the ELSR principles are compelling and that most people recognize their benefits to individuals and organizations, disagreements are inevitable and indeed necessary. We would worry about any campus that goes through this community thinking without disagreement as to content. We would expect less disagreement about the values that inform the process: respect, inclusion and openness.

Planning and implementing an education for leadership and social responsibility should be organized with reference to at least four general areas where the education will be manifest — directly in three, which are the subjects of subsequent chapters; indirectly in one (governance), which is discussed in this chapter. We mention the first three here only for conceptual purposes, since their content will be discussed at length later.

1   *An integrated curriculum and co-curriculum.*   The learning experiences — in a variety of forms, in and out of the classroom — make available the content of inclusive leadership and social responsibility.

2   *Methods of teaching and learning.*   The process of teaching and learning provides the relationships and opportunities to practice inclusive leadership and social responsibility.

3   *Institutional governance.*   How the institution conducts itself — treats people, makes decisions, plans, formulates and implements policy — is a significant part of the context from which students learn about inclusive leadership and social responsibility.

4   *Links to the community.*   Programs with partners in the community beyond the campus provide leadership learning and model social responsibility.

Each of these broad areas will need to formulate:

- a statement of objectives which can be operationalized for measurement;
- work plans that provide implementation time lines and personnel responsibilities;
- budget and spending plans which coordinate with work plans;
- evaluation and feedback plans.

(Table 5.1 provides a sample work plan as illustration.)

Although timetables need to be laid out for various objectives (success being ultimately measured in new programs, courses, teaching strategies, skills, assessment procedures — see Chapter 8), predicting when comprehensive institutional change will be integrated into the college culture is problematic. Some institutions are in the second half of a decade of implementing the quality revolution on their campuses (Wolverton, 1994).

Planning and implementing new ideas and new programs will occur simultaneously on many levels within the organization: within schools, colleges or divisions, driven by specific subject area missions; within departments, with attention to particular majors; by individuals, with attention to professional development and community outreach. Obviously

Table 5.1:   *Sample work plan component: Curriculum and co-curriculum*

Activity	Timeline	Person(s) responsible	Resources	Outcomes	Evaluation criteria (see Evaluation Plan)
Development of 'In Community' courses	FY97: J F M A M x x x	two faculty	course reductions (one per semester)	two courses approved by Curriculum Committee	students enrolled
Plan and supervise four-year leadership program	Planning: FY97: J F M A M Implement: FY97: S O N D	one faculty and Assistant Dean	one course reduction per semester for faculty	Curriculum and co-curriculum program for 100 students	activities and attitudes of students

those most closely associated with various areas will be most involved in their planning and implementation, but consideration of all areas should involve a variety of campus (and sometimes off-campus) constituencies. A long tradition of faculty committees, the source of many jokes, supports the culture necessary for cross-divisional teamwork, despite territorial and discipline boundaries. On most campuses, faculty committees that deal with institutional policy and legislative matters are composed of members from various disciplines to assure representation of 'different points of view and interest'. The challenge is to extend team membership beyond faculty to include representation from all parts of the community and to maintain a focus on the vision of the graduate in the course of committee conversations.

As the process of planning proceeds, new ideas and programs will be proposed to improve upon the processes and operations that are being reviewed. Implementation of new ideas should be left as much to the local level as possible. Individuals, especially those who have not had leadership roles in the past, should be asked to oversee and guide some facet of the change. A disengaged faculty member in Chemistry is asked to head up a proposed system to track student absences. He reluctantly accepts and is renewed as the responsibility puts him in touch with people in the system whose names he barely knew. A department secretary is asked to act on her own suggestion and organize regular meetings for department secretaries — never held before — to talk about ways to improve services to students. A human resources manager is asked to look at ways the institution might provide more opportunities to elicit ideas for ways to work more productively and cooperatively.

It is important to keep the community informed about progress being made by their colleagues in implementing new programs and ideas. A newsletter, email bulletins, occasional lunches and awards are all appropriate ways to keep the community focused on the work of education for leadership and social responsibility and to honor the accomplishments.

Organization and Governance

Inclusive leadership can be used as the organizing principle from which change, and ultimately increased learning, can flow. Planning for an education for leadership and social responsibility must include the structures and processes of the institution where the education will take place. While faculty will be primarily responsible for curriculum revision, the entire institution needs to examine the values which govern how people work and learn together. This discussion should be placed in the context of its importance in producing an environment for learning about leadership and social responsibility. It is critical that the institution reflects the values and processes of inclusive leadership in how it goes about its business.

Each functional unit — the mailroom, physical plant people, the security force, secretaries, faculty, student life, development, admissions and financial aid, students in all of their diversity — must think through its own relationship to the success of the mission of teaching and learning for inclusive leadership. The key questions to be addressed include: 'How does what we do and the way we do it impact on creating an environment of inclusive leadership, an environment that will help promote the educational goals of inclusive leadership and social responsibility?'; 'What values are reflected in the way we make decisions and the way we treat and are treated by others?'

A cross-functional group should examine the organization and governance procedures with the goal of pinpointing contradictions between the principles of inclusive leadership and the way the institution is organized for decision-making and service delivery. A major focus of planning should be to bring consistency between the way the organization runs on a daily basis and the skills and perspectives we are trying to impart to students. 'What does our structure say about our values?'; 'How do the implicit and explicit curriculums compare?' (Astin, 1988); 'What do students learn by observing and participating in the business of the institution?'

Although specific curriculum goals may not be articulated when these questions are first asked, preliminary discussion should have underscored agreement on student-centeredness and inclusive leadership principles of collaboration, democratic processes, and common good thinking. Using these principles, groups can be asked to examine the continuity of values expressed in such vital processes as collective bargaining and/or contract negotiations; Human Resources policies; hiring, promotion and tenure review processes; the budget making process; collegiality among departments; student government and the operation of other student organizations; involvement of students in decision-making; boundaries and hierarchies that mark divisions and keep people apart; classroom teaching/learning methodologies.

Collective bargaining, for example, can be transformed into collaborative bargaining if both 'sides' agree to reshape the rules, exhibit respect and trust, allow for informal communication and thinking about the common good. The budget-making process — often tightly controlled, secretive and non-participatory — can be reshaped to resemble open, community-wide planning (Chabotar, 1995). Students are often prohibited from participating in departmental decisions about curriculum and other matters. Inviting them in as collaborators, as regular members of department or other committees, would be more consistent with the inclusive leadership we are trying to impart. Is the student government an open and democratic forum or has it been taken over by a small group with authoritarian methods?

After several months of deliberations by both same-function and cross-function groups, an elected steering committee will seek to find commonality in the language and issues that different groups are expressing. The exercise might be divided into two parts; an examination of the real — how a particular process actually operates now, and the ideal — how we would like it to be.

Obstacles to Planning and Implementing Change

There are several expectable but not insurmountable obstacles that will be associated with the creation of campus wide planning for and implementation of an education for leadership and social responsibility. These concerns are linked to the national issues cited earlier, and can be anticipated on most college campuses.

- The fear that the time involved in doing the thinking, talking and listening will take away from other activities. This is an accurate assessment and this reality will underscore the importance that those in supervisory positions are placing on the process. To emphasize that participation in planning and implementation is an important part of one's job, supervisors need to help people prioritize their work in order to partici-pate. Obviously, if those in supervisory positions — from the president and administrative managers to tenured faculty — are not persuaded of the importance of the work of collabora-tive planning, it will not be successful.

- The fear of a political agenda attached to value-based educa-tion. The traditional notion of value-free education needs to be addressed and shown to be a myth. Education is always filled with values, from the selection of course content to the selec-tion of a president, to the selection of students. The framework of education for leadership and social responsibility makes the values explicit.

- The politics of campus life is often less ideological than prac-tical, as departments and individuals worry about their turf, their courses, their teaching loads, their jobs. These are real concerns made all the more predictable in times of 'academic restructuring', often the academic equivalent to 'corporate down-sizing'.

- The assumption that effective planning and significant change need to be supported by significant funding that the institu-tion doesn't have — Why start something we can't complete? This is a real Catch 22. Without the energy and passion that collaborative planning inspires, it is difficult to convince out-siders (foundations, corporations, alumni) to provide resources. A community-produced vision that responds to realities in the world has much more appeal to potential supporters than no vision or a vision that belongs to the president and the govern-ing board. The marketing appeal of a comprehensive educa-tional approach to both potential students and their parents is also a signi-ficant revenue consideration for all institutions that depend on tuition dollars for support.

- Other obstacles are associated with resistance to any kind of change from those who do not feel safe in their current posi-tions ('Will this mean downsizing and a loss of my job?'); those who feel inadequate to contribute to the process ('What do I know about the twenty-first century? I'm just a secretary.'); those who are cynical about the chances for real change ('Every few years there is another fad.') It is incumbent on leadership at all levels of the organization to deal with these responses. The most effective means is by involving the individuals in small but significant ways in the process, asking for advice and opinion, and providing a forum for the expression of their concerns. If the president and board and a majority of faculty and staff support the vision, it will be implemented successfully despite a recalcitrant minority that prefers the traditional hierarchy ('Don't put the inmates in charge.') Dissenters are in fact a necessary part of the environment that will educate for leadership and social responsibility.

We believe that the imperatives for change combined with the growth opportunities and value of the planning process itself will outweigh the obs-tacles for most people. We also acknowledge that no social process will include 100 per cent of the population, especially in an academic environment characterized historically by autonomy and by traditional power relationships.

In Chapter 6 we turn to the faculty. As leaders teaching leadership, they are the key ingredient in the recipe for change.

Chapter 6

Teachers as Leaders/Teaching for Leadership

From Faculty:

> It's my job to cover the material in the book. Let someone else worry about leadership.

> I didn't get a Ph.D to teach leadership. I'm a biologist.

> We don't have enough money in the department budget to buy the computer equipment we need. How can we afford to give resources to faculty development for teaching leadership?

The success of any educational reform depends on the energy, commitment and expertise of the faculty who, in interaction with students, will create, transmit and embody the principles of the reform. Whatever is right with American higher education is most likely a result of faculties who commit themselves to changes that will improve learning for their students. From a student-centered learning perspective, the student–teacher relationship is undoubtedly the single most important relationship on the college campus.

As discussed in the previous chapter, if an education for leadership and social responsibility is to be built, the involvement of faculty in planning it is essential. The early stages of planning fundamental reform will be spent articulating, listening, consulting and, finally, crafting an institutional statement of purpose and vision. For those who decide to create an education for leadership and social responsibility, the process will include an exploration of the concept and meaning of leadership and the resulting vision of the graduate possessing the requisite skills, perspectives and abilities to support inclusive leadership in all arenas. The vision then is revisited on a regular basis, informed by evaluation of outcomes (See Chapter 8).

An exploration of leadership, which will involve all campus groups, should be lead by the faculty. It will be guided by the following broad topics:

- discussion, if not agreement, on the *realities that will shape the twenty-first century*;
- characteristics of *twenty-first century workplaces, communities and families*;
- endorsement of the need for *common good thinking within diversity*;
- the *elements of a new kind of leadership* to respond to these realities.

Out of this exploration will come the vision of what a student needs to know and be able to do in order to participate in and promote a new kind of leadership. Our vision of Leadership Learning Goals, stated in full in Chapter 5, includes the abilities to:

- understand and use values
- appreciate cultures
- tolerate ambiguity
- communicate interpersonally
- do systems thinking
- analyze a common good
- manage and reduce conflict
- problem-find and solve
- take risks, be flexible and innovate
- trust others, collaborate in teams
- work in horizontal organizations
- find and use resources

This vision — stated as leadership learning goals — drives the need for faculty development or, more accurately, for faculty learning and preparation for creativity. What do the faculty need and need to do in order to assure the successful attainment of the learning goals by students?

Content and Process

Many refer to the curriculum as the content of learning and the methods of teaching and learning as the process. Typically, the first place an educator will look for the material that will assure the attainment of learning by students is to the structured curriculum. What courses will teach about the importance of diversity? Which department is responsible for interpersonal skills? Do we need an interdisciplinary course to help students learn how to find the common good?

Teachers who are sensitive to their role as leaders in the classroom, school or campus will also understand that the process of teaching and learning is itself a great transmitter of substance about leadership and social responsibility. Each of the leadership learning goals we have specified can be taught through the processes of learning in every classroom, regardless of subject matter. They can be learned in many other ways as well, outside of the classroom.

The curriculum, integrated with the co-curriculum, is such an important influence on the student (and on the faculty) that we devote the next chapter to it. We will focus in this chapter on some suggestions for helping faculty create learning environments, composed of both relationships and experiences, to help students observe, practice and learn about inclusive leadership and social responsibility.

Following the establishment of Leadership Learning Goals, faculty discussion of how to create the learning environment might begin with a review of the idea of teacher as leader. Many faculty will resist the notion that their behavior and the environment they create in the classroom is a direct and powerful influence on student perceptions of leadership and on the attainment of most of the leadership learning goals. The resistance is usually based on the fear of responsibility for learning outcomes that are not directly related to the course content as measured by test grades and coverage of the syllabus. Faculty need to take across the curriculum responsibility for the learning goals.

Using the Leadership Learning Goals, faculty might be asked to evaluate how the experience of their classrooms, *excluding course content*, contributes to the attainment of these goals by students. Using the list of outcomes suggested by our discussion of leadership, faculty would ask, 'How does the way we go about teaching/learning contribute to the students' ability to apply values, to appreciate culture, to develop interpersonal skills, to do systems thinking and to conceptualize a common good, to problem-find and solve and take risks, to trust others and actively participate, to find and use resources — particularly technological resources, to value diversity and work in horizontal teams?'

Systems Thinking about the Classroom

Consideration of questions like these must begin with a recognition that the classroom is a set of relationships. Like all relationships, those in the classroom are governed by values and rules. The relationships may be more or less healthy for the individuals involved, measuring health by the attainment of particular goals and general humane interactions that support growth. Though these relationships are part of a larger system — the department, college or university and American higher education generally — there is enough flexibility within the roles of faculty and student that the participants can fashion their own values and rules within the constraints of the larger system. Of course, it is also true that changes from within a system can overwhelm older ways of doing things and present new choices. So if many classes on a college campus are student-centered, interactive and collaborative, with on-going and all-around evaluation, the larger system will begin to change. Given that more than 70 per cent of classes in American universities and colleges still rely on the traditional lecture format (Gilbert, 1996), interactive classes are likely to be seen as different and perhaps by some as questionable. However, as evidence accumulates that collaborative, active learning produces better learning results, they will be valued by students and emulated by other instructors.

Ultimately faculty and students should come to see the interdependence of their roles and embrace the reality that individuals can move in and out of them, even within the bounds of the classroom. Hence another question for faculty: 'In my classroom, how do the students become teachers and how do I, the designated teacher, become a learner?' Many techniques now exist to involve students as teachers and mentors to other students. Collaborative learning is based on the perception and actuality of mutual interdependence: my success (at learning) is your success (Johnson et al., 1991; Bruffee, 1995).

While techniques are rapidly developing to increase collaborative learning among students, it is much more difficult to convince participants that the faculty member is also a learner in the classroom. As pointed out by others (Beckman, 1990), as long as teachers have the ultimate power of evaluation through the assignment of grades, the hierarchy of power remains, no matter how much we try as teachers to enter the learning process. Differences, some of which carry unequal power, do persist in our social relationships. The ability to collaborate, to create environments that reduce if not eliminate fear is critical to socially responsible leadership. If we wait to collaborate until there is a perception of complete equality, we will continue to hold on to caste-like relationships of stylized interaction and the lack of participation from those with less power. Moving into successful collaboration across power differentials may well help to loosen the social boundaries that separate people. Lack of collaboration will add to the rigidity of the boundaries and reinforce the inequality.

As part of a faculty development program, faculty should challenge themselves to make their own learning objectives specific for each course or semester. For example, in any or all of the classes they will teach in a semester can they:

- increase their ability to listen by allowing more feedback from students?
- use 360° feedback at several points during the semester, allowing students to evaluate themselves, each other and the teacher?
- obtain from their students six new ideas for better teaching?
- learn all the names of all of their students within three weeks?
- develop a portfolio approach to evaluation?
- turn some responsibility for classroom learning over to students?
- have students create examination questions and answer them?
- make explicit the values that are promoted in the course?
- learn four things from a colleague that can be incorporated into the course?

(and many more that can be generated by faculty and students).

Students and faculty tend to think in terms of the extrinsic rewards that result from the classroom experience. Teachers earn money and status and students earn another three credits toward the diploma that will increase their earning power and their status. Without denying this reality, another needs to be introduced, namely the intrinsic rewards of a 14-week, three-hour a week relationship called a class. Spending some time thinking about increasing everyone's intrinsic rewards is a worthwhile exercise which also has application in the workplace. Beyond the credits and the paycheck, what are we really getting or do we want to get out of this?

The analysis of the classroom as a social system needs to involve the students. Traditional student–teacher role expectations will get in the way of attempts to increase student responsibility for course content, non-competitive student relations and faculty learning. All of these seem contrary to normal expectations that the teacher will be in charge, will decide what is done on a minute-to-minute, class-to-class basis and will have the ultimate power of the grade. This traditional model of leadership is supported by most students and faculty and most colleges and universities. It reaffirms the perceptions of the fourth and fifth graders who spoke of the (unrealistic even in their minds) expectation that leaders need to know everything, take care of everyone and always have the right answers; moreover, leaders are mean and bossy and don't get the best out of people.

Traditional classroom hierarchies are not appropriate environments for teaching and learning about horizontal organizations, teamwork and communication. The artists who spoke in Chapter 4 would also say these are not environments conducive to creativity. In authoritarian classrooms, where the teacher is defined as the font of all wisdom, the communication is largely one way — from teacher to student, or too often from teacher into space. Gross inequalities of status and power impede two-way communication, even on email if participants are known to each other.

Likewise, the traditional model of students as passive receptors and regurgitators of what they have heard and read doesn't promote the leadership learning goals; nor will competitive relationships with classmates. If the class is organized around a win–lose grading strategy (rather than an assumption that everyone can learn the material and the success of each student enriches the learning of all) or if students see their job as scoring the most points with the teacher, other students will only be viewed as getting in the way of the attempt to be number one. In a competitive system, many, particularly those who are accustomed to feeling marginal, drop out of the competition for grades and teacher attention (Kohn, 1986; Sizer, 1992). Students need to be able to realize the potential they offer one another as resources to get the work done and as supporters of collective learning.

A systems analysis of the classroom will also illuminate the feedback and reward structure and will allow participants to brainstorm about how they might build in continuous feedback — student-to-student, teacher-to-student (individual and group) and student-to-teacher. Clearly the traditional combination of midterm, final exam, and term paper will not suffice if the objective is to create continuous learning and improvement and to open communication. Techniques for increasing continuous assessment may range from email communication to anonymous statements ('the most important thing I learned today was . . .') submitted at the end of each class; to focus groups facilitated by a visiting faculty member that address 'how I learn best in this class', to peer evaluations of work in progress. Many more ideas can be generated by the participants in the class.

Using a systems model of the classroom not only illuminates the structural traps that teachers and students may be caught in, but it is also a good opportunity to strengthen one of the leadership learning goals — the ability to think systemically and holistically.

As faculty take on the characteristics of inclusive leadership in the classroom they will also provide a better environment for learning the content of their course. Students will be more engaged in and have ownership for the outcome of the class experience. By becoming teachers themselves, students will be increasing the supply of teaching available. They should more readily break the time and space boundaries of the classroom and communicate with each other outside of class, in study groups, on email or by phone. The teacher as leader will make it clear that this kind of communication is valued and will seek to be included in out-of-classroom communication.

Faculty who begin to consciously model inclusive leadership in the classroom will need the on-going support of colleagues who are attempting the same. Regular meetings to share successes and failures will be essential to sustain the pioneers and to draw more colleagues into the discussion. Public recognition, including the possibility of monetary rewards, for the attempts — not necessarily only the successes, will go a long way to acknowledge the institutional commitment to change.

Delivery

As Ernest Boyer (1990) argued persuasively, we need to look at scholarship as a broad set of activities that includes those directly related to the improvement of curriculum and to the understanding of teaching and learning. Boyer's definition needs little extension to encompass the activities of the teacher in the role of leader organizing the classroom and the activities to maximize learning. The educator's professional responsibility is to create appropriate vehicles for the delivery of the content of his or her field. While the professor as scholar contributes to the knowledge that exists in the field, the professor as educator is also responsible for ensuring that the knowledge is understandable and useable by the undergraduate student and, hopefully, by the public. Thus the teacher as leader will heed the words of the fourth grade boy who advised leaders that 'If people are confused, don't leave them confused.'

What follows are some ideas that might be employed to assist faculty to think about the broad framework of inclusive leadership and social responsibility and their leadership role as teachers. Ideally, ideas for faculty development will spring from the faculty as they identify their own needs. The identification of a faculty member as faculty development coordinator will help to locate and coordinate efforts and provide a visible center for resources available to faculty and staff. A number of development opportunities should be available to appeal to the variety of needs and predispositions that will be apparent in any faculty. Not all members of a faculty will take advantage of all the opportunities, but few should miss being involved in some aspect of faculty development to help the institution produce the necessary learning climate.

Intensive Workshop for Faculty: Teachers as Leaders/ Teaching for Leadership

What follows is a sample that can be restructured to fit the needs of a particular campus. It includes the key components that need to be addressed by a faculty preparing to deliver an education for leadership and social responsibility. All of the components can stand alone as full or half-day workshops or can constitute a semester or year long series of programs.

The objective is to introduce faculty and staff to an ELSR framework, improve the framework through their participation, and provide resources for faculty to use in their courses. The method of instruction should model interactive learning and teaching.

Day One: A Framework for Thinking About Leadership

1 What are the realities of the twenty-first century world in which our students will lead?
   Team activity. Working in teams, participants formulate their concepts of the most pressing realities of the twenty-first century. A master list with common themes will be drawn from team contributions.
2 What holds us together in the face of diversity and differing opinions?
   Simulation: The Prisoner's Dilemma (Axelrod, 1984) This simulation should provoke a discussion of the tension between decentralization and the common good as well as a recognition of the role of trust as the foundation of human relationships.
3 Exclusive and Inclusive Leadership.
   Memories. Share memories of how you learned about leadership as a child. Sometimes these are contained in family myths and folklore, often they are found in recollections of school and church and peer group experiences. Were early formulations confirmed or reshaped by adult experiences, for example, in the military, the family, in college and graduate school, etc.?
   Draw a picture of leadership. A small group exercise with no further instruction. Pictures are shared and explained to the larger group. The experience of the leaderless group to get the work done might also be discussed. What are the models of leadership we present everyday on this campus for our students? Follow with a discussion of exclusive, traditional leadership

and its contrast with inclusive leadership. What are the value bases and assumptions of each?

4 The Practical Side of Inclusive Leadership.
Content analysis. Participants will consult periodicals such as *Fortune, Business Week, New York Times,* and *Forbes* for evidence of workplace themes forecasting the qualities of leadership needed for the twenty-first century workplace and community. Discussion can be extended to characteristics of the twenty-first century classroom.

Day Two: Leadership and Creativity

Through an exploration of creativity, participants clarify the characteristics of inclusive leadership and how to cultivate them.

Brainstorming exercise. Contrast the stereotypic characteristics of children and adults to demonstrate the dulling of creativity in adults.

Create a culture. In groups of five or six, participants are given bags filled with assorted items (found in desk drawers, children's toy boxes, junk drawers and magazines) and asked to describe the nature of the culture from which these artifacts were obtained. This exercise provides a vehicle for discussion of the conditions that facilitate and impede creativity. It also provides for reflection on the leadership that was demonstrated in the group as it mobilized to get the work done.

Conversations with artists. Community or campus artists are invited to speak about the work they do and how they do it. Following the conversation with several artists, faculty and staff try to relate the content of the discussions to their own work and to the process of leadership and to learning.

In processing all these activities, factors that impede and facilitate creativity and leadership in students and in teachers should be inventoried.

Day Three: Teaching and Practicing Inclusive Leadership in the Classroom

Systems analysis of the classroom. In small groups, using large paper, draw the classroom as a system. What are the parts, the relationships and flow of communication among parts? How can the system be improved? Compare drawings.

Interactive and reflective teaching and learning.   Role play:

- The exclusive teacher, student and curriculum
- The inclusive teacher, student and curriculum

Describe a hypothetical class that models inclusive leadership and one that models traditional leadership. What are the pros and cons of each?

Brainstorming on interactive teaching strategies.   These may be presented more fully in future workshops:

- Journal keeping
- Case studies
- Simulations
- Teaching to diverse learning styles

- Student-constructed course syllabi
- Collaborative learning strategies
- Student peers as teachers
- Evaluation techniques

The linkage of all these techniques to teaching for inclusive leadership should be made clear. Abundant resources are available to document the increases in learning that take place when students have more voice and responsibility for their own learning as well as the learning of others (Johnson et al., 1991, 1994).

Following this three-day intensive workshop, smaller groups of faculty should be encouraged to pursue spin-off groups that meet for further discussion. These are especially important to allow faculty to propose the introduction of new approaches in their classes, to know that colleagues in different subject areas are trying the same things and to report back on their experiences.

Integrative Seminars

Two seminars undergird this experience offered for about 20 faculty each semester. Figure 6.1 suggests an organization of subject matter and participants into interactive experiences over time. It is best to begin this series with a planning group in the fall semester and the first series of seminars starting in the spring semester.

Two seminars form the core for discussion about educating for leadership and social responsibility. One, *Foundations in Leadership for the Common Good*, explores the classical roots and current applications of the values that support inclusive leadership and decision-making in the common interest. A second seminar, *Understanding Continuity and*

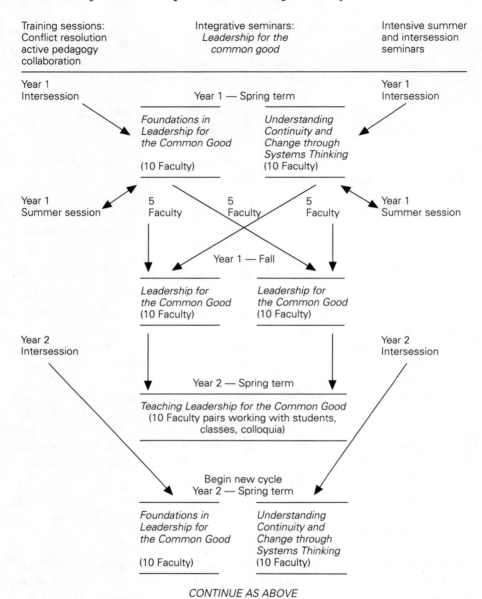

Figure 6.1: Faculty development seminars

Change Through Systems Thinking, reviews the application of systems analysis to local, national and global interdependencies, to cultural diversity and inequality, to the social impact of technology, and to complex organizations.

Following a semester of conversation, the faculty participants use the summer to explore either conflict resolution or active learning techniques. In the following semester, five faculty from each of the two original seminars form two new seminars, thereby cross-fertilizing *foundations* and *systems.* Several participants will either have been through teaching workshops or have been trained in conflict resolution during the summer. These integrative seminars will connect the foundational concepts about the common good and inclusive leadership with systems thinking, conflict resolution and active-learning strategies.

In Year 2, the original participants team up to disseminate their insights and strategies in classes, colloquiums or other forums. More faculty begin the process as participants in the original seminars and the cycle continues as long as there is interest.

Other Strategies for Faculty Development

Faculty and staff fund. A pool of money or time (course release) to support faculty initiatives to promote an ELSR. These resources should be distributed by a committee of faculty and staff who read proposals and decide on the relative merits of investing in new ideas. Amounts of support may be modest but will help spark the creation of ideas and active participation. Proposals generated by and involving more than one individual, including students, should be most favorably evaluated both because they will encourage collaboration and will have a broader impact.

Collaborative seminars. Composed of faculty, students, and community people, these seminars are formed around a topic of broad interest such as the local environment, women's health, creativity and the workplace, improving local education. The group decides on an agenda with a small budget for resources and outside speakers. Each seminar is required to produce a collaborative product that can be utilized in the community and/or by the college. A teaching module for business or classroom use, a resource directory, a simulation game for educational purposes, a video or a poetry collection are examples of useable product outcomes of the seminar's collaborative efforts.

Three-year development programs for faculty. A plan of activities to meet the objectives of ELSR, composed by the faculty member in consultation with a peer committee. Plans may include course development or revision, attendance at conferences, integration of collaborative teaching techniques, development of partnerships with the community, etc. Progress is reviewed once a year and encouragement and redirection given as necessary to the success of the plan. A stipend of time or money is awarded (or banked) for successful completion of the plan, which may be re-entered after a one-year hiatus.

Conflict resolution workshops and training. This is provided for faculty and members of all sectors of the institution. (The organization of this initiative is discussed fully in Chapter 7.) A major benefit of the conflict resolution workshops is the opportunity for faculty to work with members of the college community from a variety of departments. As campus security, secretaries, student life, students and housekeeping staff interact with faculty around issues of mutual concern, the building of community is fostered. As the program develops, campus people will be trained to carry on the training. An established Conflict Resolution Center on campus allows students, staff and faculty opportunities to practice and to utilize the techniques to resolve on-campus problems. Those trained in the processes can offer services to the community for the resolution of conflict.

Peer teaching coaches. Faculty pair up to be observers in one another's classes. The observer makes a commitment to attend at least 30 per cent of the classes in any semester. Both the teacher and the observer hold conversations with small groups of students at an early, mid and later point in the semester to find out *how* students are learning in the class and to gauge student response to active learning techniques that are being used. Students are asked to reflect on their own learning. To what conditions are they most responsive? When do they feel most intellectually open and responsive? By recalling specific examples from both in and outside of the classroom, students will raise their own awareness as well as the awareness of the instructor as to their learning styles. Observer and teacher will share impressions in their own conversations. Sometime during the semester, the coaching teams can meet as a group to share what they have learned about student learning styles and effective teaching strategies. Others not participating in the program can be invited to attend these discussions as well. (This suggestion is derived from the model used by the New Jersey Master Teacher's Program.)

Interdepartmental sabbaticals. Cultivating interdisciplinary thinking is central to developing the flexibility of mind required for creativity and problem-solving. Faculty can apply to a faculty committee for the opportunity to reduce by one-half or by 100 per cent their regular teaching load in order to spend the released time with a department other than their own. The individual would become a participating member of the other department, auditing classes, joining in discussion and problem-solving about department business and sharpening a new perspective. Course revision or development to reflect interdisciplinary thinking can be an expected outcome of the sabbatical. Not only do interdepartmental sabbaticals produce intellectual links among the faculty, these cross-cutting affiliations also model the kind of networked organization the institution should be striving to become.

Obstacles and Facilitators to Teachers as Leaders

This chapter has outlined the need for a dramatic shift in thinking and behavior for faculty. If we remember that faculty are deeply grounded in the disciplines of their degrees, trained as researchers, scholars, writers, artists and scientists, the expectations of the teachers as leaders framework are even more ambitious. The dominant model of the academic professor does not demand much interaction with students or even knowledge of students and the learning process. It is a professor-centered or knowledge-centered approach that sees the teaching role as secondary and limited to dispenser of information. The information is assumed to be intrinsically interesting, students are assumed to be internally motivated to learn, and the lecture format is assumed to be the fastest, most efficient form of knowledge dissemination.

During the past 20 years, academics have been asked to do more. They have been asked to turn themselves into real human beings in the classroom — teachers, in interaction with students. They have been asked to care about whether their students learn, to understand the learning process and to consider alternative delivery methods. Further, they have been asked to reactivate their own role as learner.

Students have also been asked to change. Traditionally, for more than a dozen years before they get to college, students have received praise and good grades (success) for being the passive recipient of incoming information. The goal of the school game was to figure out what the teacher wanted and give it to him or her. This is in stark contrast to the Leadership Learning Goals we have set out for students.

To the extent that traditional student–faculty roles prevail, and in most places they do, crafting an education for leadership and social responsibility will be difficult. The role relationship between teacher and student is one of power and dependency, with reliance on power to get things done. Communication is limited, stylized and one-way;

few processes are available for two-way communication, and few opportunities for risk-taking and failure. Moreover, the relationship among students is governed by the principles of competition, which militate against cooperation. Finally, the time and space restriction imposed by current academic schedules and structures limits the possibilities for relationships to flourish.

These limitations are not insurmountable. Teachers and students, within the confines of their classroom or as part of a system-wide approach, can consciously seek to redefine their roles. The hierarchy will not disappear entirely, but it can be diminished as learners take more responsibility for group learning and teachers become coaches and mentors — inclusive leaders. The redefinition of roles will emphasize the interdependencies — teacher-to-student, student-to-student, and, in some cases of collaborative teaching, teacher-to-teacher. These interdependencies require bringing the student into the process of teaching and the teacher into the process of learning. Time and place restrictions can be broken as classroom experiences are carried outside of class, using work groups, community-based projects, and email.

Successful faculty development efforts will energize and empower the faculty to turn their attention — as we do now — to the core of the student experience, the curriculum and the co-curriculum, where the ideas generated in faculty development will come alive for the students.

Chapter 7

An Integrated Learning Experience: The Curriculum and Co-curriculum

From faculty and staff:

> Didn't we just redo our general education courses a few years ago? Why do we need to do it again?

> On my campus the faculty rarely speak to the student life staff. They think all we do is arrange volleyball games.

> We have an abundance of activities on campus but just a small group of the same students participate.

While the ELSR framework requires an institution to be student-centered in all of its operations and assumptions, it remains the responsibility of the faculty to award degrees and to certify student competencies. A commitment to educate for leadership and social responsibility makes that responsibility very pointed. At the same time, everyone who works for the institution shares some responsibility for assisting students in achieving leadership learning goals.

In order for this across-the-campus approach to work, the learning goals must be explicitly stated and understood by all members of the campus community. (Alverno College in Wisconsin is an outstanding example of institution-wide clarity and commitment to student learning.) Leadership learning goals may be posted on office walls and appear in publications, speeches, and in course syllabi as a reminder to students, staff and faculty of the purposes for their being at the institution.

Sample Abbreviated Form of Leadership Learning Goals for Widespread Campus Distribution

Leadership Learning Goals:
Components of an education for leadership and social responsibility and how we work at _____ college/university.

- *Ways of looking*: Systems and common good thinking
- *Ways of learning and doing*: Collaboration, teams, creativity, risk-taking, flexibility; trust
- *Ways of Understanding*: Culture, values, and aesthetics; problem-finding and solving, including conflict resolution; resource literacy; communication

---

Breaking Boundaries

On most college campuses today, faculty responsibility for curriculum, standards and degree granting is acknowledged and fiercely guarded. Without doubt these responsibilities need to stay with those who have devoted their lives to the understanding, acquisition and transmission of knowledge. The challenge of an ELSR is therefore not for faculty to relinquish that control but to share responsibility for the education of students with those not trained to be academics. For historical and structural reasons, this will not be easy.

If we are to achieve a student-centered education for leadership and social responsibility and if the institution is to model less rigidity among its parts, serious attention must be paid to the existing boundaries among divisions and the people within them. All offices and divisions of the institution should be integrated around the leadership learning goals and their application for both current students and for the constituencies with which the office has most contact (alumni, corporations, foundations, parents, legislators, community groups). The goals should also find application for the staff in all division offices, across which a consistent message about institutional goals and values is crucial. Each office must ask, 'How can the learning goals of current students be enhanced by the work of this office?' and 'How do the learning goals apply to the people who work in this office and how we go about our work? Do we need help to achieve some of the goals?'

Offices should consciously seek to involve other departments/

divisions in their work as members of planning groups and on assignments to special projects. A phone call from one office to another, requesting the assistance of a member of that office on a project or in a brainstorming session, should be warmly received and supported by supervisors. This cross-fertilization helps to keep the whole organization on one center — student success — and to increase efficiency (Lawler, 1992; Sayles, 1993; Johnson and Johnson, 1994).

A student-centered institution will promote boundary crossing within the organization. Offices which have hitherto seemed extraneous to student learning — alumni affairs, development, external relations, physical plant, admissions — become part of the whole effort to promote learning outcomes, as the staff of these offices discuss how they can help. Suggestions might include:

- involving students in the work of the office as paid or volunteer workers: assisting them with a systems view of the operations of the office; involving them in collaborative problem-solving; providing opportunities to practice communication skills and to practice leadership;
- involving students as interns with course-specific learning assignments;
- modeling for students' collaborative work relationships and common good thinking;

A learner-centered approach sees the potential for learning everywhere and understands the role of everyone as an educator.

The Academic–Student Life Divide

One of the most persistent boundaries on campuses has been between Academic Affairs and Student Life. Critical to the success of ELSR is not just bridging this traditional divide, but integrating the work of the two divisions. For not only is there now a separation of function; there is also a distinct hierarchy between those in student life and the faculty. Student life personnel and activities are often disparaged by faculty as soft, without the rigorous learning that faculty can provide in the classroom. The status differential is underscored by the prestige accorded the Ph.D which is held by most faculty. This hierarchy reflects a faculty-centered (and to a lesser extent staff-centered) institution. A student-centered approach requires both divisions to provide the best learning opportunities available for the student. From the student's point of view, learning is not dependent on a particular place or category of people. It results from relationships and access to resources that can easily cross institutional boundaries.

On most campuses, what passes for leadership education has been the province of student life, with little respect bestowed on it by the faculty. Given this history, leadership is usually associated with the running of meetings and the mobilization of activities for clubs or community volunteer programs. Campus leaders are those in formal positions in student organizations. Leadership development is generally aimed at a small number of students who are active on the campus. No academic content is expected.

As faculty take ownership for the preparation of students for leadership and social responsibility and proceed with the work of building the curriculum, they will need to work with student life staff in true colleagueship to attain the leadership learning goals they desire for their students. Both divisions will appreciate the overlap of content, skills and the abilities they are trying to achieve and will seek to tie the co-curriculum more closely with the curriculum. From the student's viewpoint, the coherence will reinforce learning.

As students move through their undergraduate experience, we want to assure that they have repeated opportunities to explore and experience the dimensions of inclusive leadership in the curriculum and co-curriculum. Not every student will be exposed to every program; but all students, regardless of major, will have multiple opportunities to develop the leadership learning goals. We turn first to the general curriculum.

ELSR in the Disciplines

A comfortable place for most faculty to begin is with their own disciplines. Collaborating with one another and external consultants, faculty can examine the curriculum to determine the contributions made by their fields to an understanding of inclusive leadership and social responsibility. Faculty from related disciplines (the social sciences, humanities, natural sciences, business and professional programs) can participate together in workshops to define general directions for course and program revision. A faculty coordinator from each area may be partially released from teaching responsibilities to oversee the workshop discussions and stay in conversation with other areas. New courses can be developed and existing ones reshaped to assure an across-the-curriculum approach to these fundamental concepts. Based on discussions with faculty, we would expect the following curricular emphases, which only begin to scratch the surface of possibilities:

- *From the social sciences.*   leadership styles and the study of decision-making; community studies; power and organizational analyses; policy studies; political processes and citizenship participation; human diversity; social change; group dynamics; institutionalized inequalities; futures studies; ethics and public policy.
- *From the fine arts and humanities.*   leadership in literature; historical studies of leadership; the process of creativity; inter-personal and public communication; social ethics; cross-cultural communication; exposure to performance arts as artist and audience.
- *From the natural sciences.*   ethics in science; science and social responsibility; the process of scientific discovery; the applica-tion of scientific knowledge to human problems; technology, society, and values; environmental studies; the limits of science.
- *From the business program.*   corporate decision making; cor-porate social responsibility; ethics in business; business and the public good; democracy, creativity, and collaboration in the workplace; horizontal organizations; and teamwork in net-worked organizations.
- *From professional programs.*   professional leadership; profes-sions and public service; professional ethics and social respons-ibility; professionals as change agents; a systems approach to professional practice; and minorities and women in the professions.

In addition, each area should consider its contribution to the broad issues identified as realities of the twenty-first century: technology and values; cultural pluralism and inequality; humanizing work and service organizations; and global interdependencies.

ELSR in General Education

One of the most important functions of an ELSR is to bring coherence to the four-year undergraduate experience. The coherence should begin with those courses designated for all students to form the foundation for learning. Faculty need to rethink the general education curriculum with leadership learning goals in mind. Some institutions may develop specific general education courses to introduce inclusive leadership and the concepts associated with it. Most will want to insure that the ELSR themes and interactive methods of teaching are apparent in all general education courses. Whatever the particulars of any general education program, an ELSR will require an emphasis on interdisciplinary, team teaching, active learning and the integration of courses. Following are some suggestions for enhancing general education through ELSR:

1 A core course might introduce students to the components of inclusive leadership; to methods of analysis for systems thinking and common good thinking; and to small group collaborative problem-solving. Use of case studies involving ethical dilemmas can help sharpen values analysis. Cross-cultural examples can bring the necessary sensitivity to how collaboration, systems and common good thinking, and inclusive leadership are reinforced or undermined by particular values and different cultural traditions.

2 Several majors might collaborate on junior and senior year colloquia that bring together students with various internship experiences to address significant issues. This is especially relevant for professional programs whose graduates will work together on problems in fields like education, law enforcement, health, social service, as well as for those joining business organizations with staffs from a variety of discipline backgrounds. At a culminating colloquium, other majors are invited to participate in discussion. Several such colloquia might be organized into a conference for the entire campus.

3 A general education component in the senior year that integrates and reinforces the ELSR framework. These required courses, taken with a professor outside of the major department, use an interdisciplinary approach to illuminate a problem or issue. The student works as part of an interdisciplinary team to analyze issues (using systems and common good thinking) and develop action plans for further research or for policy development. Suggested topics might include: Community and the common good; Leadership, Public issues and social ethics; Problem-solving in multicultural communities; Profit and the common good; Pollution; Conflict resolution; Science and ethics; Communication, technology and privacy.

4 A small fund to support student initiated ideas to promote the leadership learning goals should uncover some interesting suggestions for the curriculum. Proposals might come from individuals or from student organizations which will find their own ways of manifesting inclusive leadership and social responsibility. For example, students in different courses might

be encouraged to work collaboratively to develop case studies, works of art, debates, articles, research projects and community projects that enhance their learning and contribute to a collaborative community of learners. A joint student-faculty committee would oversee, nurture and publicize projects.

The First Year Experience

Great strides have been made in the past 15 years to recognize the importance of the first year to academic and social success in college. The University of South Carolina has pioneered work which many others have adopted and modified as campuses give special attention to first-year students. Recognizing this, we suggest a few initiatives that might be directed toward incoming students.

1 A first-year experience course can introduce the expectation that all students have leadership potential and establish the link between responsible leadership and commitment to community within a multicultural environment. Racism, sexism and other social barriers among people should be explored as impediments to understanding, problem solving, and inclusive leadership. Using upper-class students as assistants in the course, first-year students can be encouraged to make connections with organizations at the college as a first step in ensuring their involvement in the college community.

2 To further enhance the coherence of the first year, a common experience three times a semester can present all members of the first-year class with issues relevant to ELSR themes. Topics might include: leadership in comparative cultures, the concept of the common good, the classical roots of leadership, alternative sustainable futures, the individual and the community, and the planetary good. The format can vary from invited speakers, to films, to interactive simulations. Faculty teaching first-year courses can draw upon these experiences for application to their particular courses. Preceding the common experiences, faculty who teach first-year courses should meet with the guest lecturer or session organizer to discuss the topic, its relevance to their classes, and methods of teaching the concepts to first-year students.

3 Often a team-building activity for first-year students helps define the nature of interdependence and the expectation for

involvement held by the campus. These activities can include challenging outdoor explorations, ropes and other obstacle courses, and simulations of situations that place survival at risk. Variations of 'The Plane Wreck' (Johnson and Johnson, 1994) create conditions of interdependence: in this exercise individuals must work cooperatively to build a vessel to catch rain water, following a plane crash that has left one person sightless and unable to speak and has left the other without use of her hands. Lessons about leadership are also learned in processing these activities.

ELSR and Diversity

At the core of inclusive leadership is the necessity for people with varied primary group identifications to work and grow together without sacrificing identity. The students who come together for education on most college campuses represent various ethnic, racial, gender and social class groups. In most cases the diversity is not as abundant as desired and, with affirmative outreach being threatened in the current political climate, that diversity may narrow even further. To prepare for the work of the twenty-first century, tomorrow's leaders need a safe place today to explore their differences together and to practice finding their common good. To the extent that campuses cannot provide an environment of diversity, the students will be less well prepared for leadership roles in democratic organizations interacting within a global community. An ELSR therefore encourages campuses to take advantage of the diversity represented, as well as to seek more. (Many programs to increase contact with diverse groups will involve community partnerships, to be discussed in Chapter 9.) Curriculum and co-curriculum ideas include the following:

1   *Big siblings.*   To increase their involvement in the life of the campus and local community, students of color can serve as big siblings to first-year students of color making contact at three points: with those who have been accepted and not yet committed; during orientation or over the summer; and in the first-year experience course. They can continue to serve as peer mentors throughout the semester, joining with staff and faculty of color to provide a network of support for the new students of color. Once support is secured (by the spring semester), the group can consider a larger common good, beyond particular group identity, and invite others to plan and implement some

college-wide program or service that benefits a wider range of people.

2 *Infusion project.* Development of a plan for systematic review of courses for opportunities for students to explore human and cultural differences and to be challenged to find common goods. Part of an infusion project might include a core course on American cultural diversity to introduce students to perspectives and empirical conclusions which describe the dimensions of human diversity and challenge commonly held stereotypes. In order to allow students to become involved in the affective dimensions of intercultural dynamics as well as the theory and research, the course might use literature, films, simulations, role playing and case studies to demonstrate the power of ethnocentrism to close minds and limit options.

3 *Grandparents in residency.* As a way of helping students explore their own ethnic origins as well as the role of gender and age in influencing life outcomes, students invite grandparents to spend a few days on campus. Bringing the grandparents together to tell their stories is a fascinating opportunity to learn about history, ethnicity and gender. The sharing among the older people can often be as valuable as the sharing between generations. In addition to exposure to ethnic differences, students can analyze the lives of the grandparents for leadership and social responsibility and for prevailing notions of a common good.

4 *Human relations workshops.* These will bring together all campus constituencies and participating teachers from local school districts to address individual and institutional discrimination and prejudice. The purpose is to promote understanding and increase communication about intercultural dynamics. These workshops are invaluable in laying the foundation of trust necessary for the school-college partnerships that we discuss in Chapter 9.

5 *Student task force on human relations and social responsibility.* This provides a vehicle for students to assume leadership roles in defining, analyzing and proposing remedies for problems on campus. Most of the human relations problems on campus reflect an absence of an adequate sense of social responsibility and ability to self govern. Issues which may be addressed by the Student Task Force include: academic dishonesty, destruction and theft of library materials, vandalism in the dormitory, date rape and intolerance for cultural differences.

ELSR in the Community

The community beyond the campus provides numerous learning opportunities for an ELSR:

1 *Courses in the community.* Beyond discipline-specific internships, courses in the community allow students to become involved with community or public agency problems and link community service with classroom discussion and analysis for academic credit. One vehicle is courses in which students from several disciplines collaborate to serve as consultants to the community and provide solutions to community problems derived from interdisciplinary perspectives. Students might study environmental problems, propose a recycling program, establish community mediation boards, explore community opinion on a political issue, try to improve 'town–gown' relations, help project future needs of the elderly.

   Other courses can be developed which use on-going experiences in the community to inform class readings and discussions. For example, a Community literacy project becomes more than community service when it is illuminated by the academic content of a sociology of education or a child psychology course. A placement at an environmental center becomes more than a volunteer activity when it is integrated into an environmental studies or chemistry of water course. Because the community work is part of a course, the expectation for attendance is high and is monitored. Students are able to share their experiences directly with others who are doing the same. Motivation to learn is generally very high in these courses, where students engage in issues with real people with whom they form relationships.

2 *Visiting public servants program.* The attempt to join commitment to social responsibility with student interest in career development suggests a need to increase student awareness of the career relevance of service in the public interest. As a partial response to that need, a visiting public servants program brings to campus individuals whose lives reflect a dedication to service on behalf of the common good. The program provides an opportunity for students and faculty to hear about the career experiences of individuals who have connected their professional interests with public service. The visitors serve as role models for students and may help faculty develop community service internships.

Public service visitors can be scheduled to come to campus for periods of two–three days during the academic year, coming, for example, from the fields of law, health, government, business, human and social services, and education. An interdisciplinary faculty committee receives recommendations, selects visitors for invitation to the campus, and organizes the visitor's schedule of activities. These activities might include:

- Presentation to the entire first-year class on a topic relevant to leadership and social responsibility. Faculty who teach first-year courses can meet with the visitor before this presentation for a discussion of the topic and how they can integrate it into the content of their own courses.
- Small group interaction with students — meals, residence hall visits, participation in classes, informal gatherings with student organizations. These opportunities will allow students to ask the public servant specific questions about academic/career preparation, career paths and work experiences.
- Meeting with department internship coordinators to discuss opportunities for student involvement in service placements.
- Participation in a collaborative seminar On the Common Good. Faculty and administrators will be involved along with representatives from the community, (such as educators, public interest lawyers, social service representatives, minority community representatives, local business people, media professionals) in a year long seminar to explore the common good. Some meetings may include participation by a visiting public servant.
- Follow-up with student visits to the workplaces of the public servants.

3 *Volunteer and public service.* Every ELSR campus should have an office of volunteer service to locate and coordinate opportunities for students and other campus members. In addition, many organizations on campus can be encouraged to add community service to their mission. An ELSR college might encourage or require community service as part of merit based financial aid awards to students.

4 *Internships.* Most majors should develop an internship course as part of the program of study. Internships provide excellent

opportunities to observe and interact with various leadership styles. Students should be challenged to compare their observations within the framework of inclusive leadership and social responsibility. In addition to other dimensions of learning, the internship should be used to test hypotheses about leadership. Students doing internships in different fields can gather during the semester to discuss the leadership dimensions of their placements.

In addition to business, departments can seek placements in public agencies and institutions which serve the larger community. Department chairs or internship coordinators may need to discuss internship development as a group in order to foster standardized procedures, to share resources and problems, and develop interdisciplinary internship projects.

Conflict Resolution

As part of the initiative to integrate the learning experience, produce socially responsible leaders and build community, all constituencies of the campus can participate in conflict resolution training. Through direct experience in conflict resolution, faculty, students and staff can build skills for responsible participation in settings from the family to the community, to the workplace, to policy arenas. Given recent calls for civility in the US Congress, conflict resolution skills may find particular relevance within our bodies of government.

A Center for Conflict Resolution can help weave the skills and the spirit of conflict resolution into the fabric of the campus. The presence of the Center will raise awareness both on and off campus of the value the institution places on the resolution approach. Workshops to introduce all members of the campus to the theory and techniques of conflict resolution help build community, as members from all campus groups learn together from similar experiences of conflict in their work settings. The workshops make clear that strategies for conflict resolution can be employed by groundskeepers, students, professors, receptionists and financial aid directors. Groups that receive some training together may remain intact as sounding boards for referral of actual cases. Video tapes of actual or simulated cases (produced by students in media and communication) can become instructional tools for the training of others. (A comprehensive undergraduate and graduate program in conflict resolution has been developed at Syracuse University.)

The Center can facilitate decentralized, informal mediation as well as provide a setting in which more formal conflict resolution and mediation can occur. It can facilitate discussion groups, conduct workshops and provide opportunities for the application of conflict resolution in the community. The Center can also serve as a resource for course development. As members of the college community learn to work more collaboratively and cross boundaries that have separated them in the past, they will gain increased confidence in their own ability to assume responsibility for a common good. An initial group of campus people, representing a cross-section of the campus, may be trained in conflict resolution by outsiders and then serve as on-campus trainers to diffuse the techniques throughout the community.

A cluster of courses that relate to conflict resolution might be developed for a certificate program that can also use the Center for internships and research. These courses might be drawn from social work, psychology, political science, sociology, education, criminal justice, and business, and include such topics as international conflict and negotiation, family and divorce mediation, community agencies and conflict resolution, the legal aspects of mediation, theories of interpersonal and group conflict, and intercultural perspectives on conflict and its resolution.

ELSR and Teacher Education

Although ELSR provides a model for professional leadership for all majors, the messages for education majors are particularly strong. The Teachers as Leaders/Teaching for Leadership component, discussed in Chapter 6 as a part of faculty development, should be offered in the curriculum for undergraduate education majors. Education courses can extend the application of teaching for inclusive leadership to kindergarten through high school. In addition, education majors will have abundant reinforcement of teachers as leaders as they interact on campus with a faculty that is modeling inclusive leadership across the college. Thus, the education of education majors becomes the responsibility of all faculty. ELSR campuses will graduate teachers prepared to take modified forms of the leadership learning goals and inclusive leadership teaching methods into their classrooms in elementary, middle and high schools.

For non-education majors, this commitment to teachers as leaders/teaching for leadership results in an increase in their awareness of the importance of teachers as change agents for more inclusive leadership.

Non-education majors should graduate with an awareness of the role they and their workplaces and communities might play to assure an education for leadership and social responsibility for the pre-college population. Hopefully, they will understand their own responsibility to become involved with schools and form partnerships to help teachers deliver the kind of education they have received.

Education majors should be afforded the opportunity to come together in an interdisciplinary colloquium with other students in professional programs to focus on their common concerns. Keeping the focus on the students they will be serving as teachers, education majors will profit from exchanges with those who will enter criminal justice, social work, health, psychology, sociology and business. A fine arts, humanities or science major who anticipates a career involving work with students would also benefit from this interdisciplinary colloquium.

The need to extend collegial boundaries to include the community beyond the campus (discussed in Chapter 9) is particularly relevant for the education program. Teachers from area schools are excellent resources for the process of curriculum revision, as mentors to students, and as sounding boards for some of the more progressive ideas in ELSR. Their involvement with the education department can begin to break down the hierarchical distinction between teachers in kindergarten through high school and those of us teaching college. Just as the teachers from the community can become resources to the college department, the college faculty and students might help a school or an entire system implement an education for leadership and social responsibility (see Chapter 9). In addition, college departments can collaborate with local school systems on grant proposals to support programs which benefit both the education majors and the children in school classes. Conferences on college campuses could promote the exchange of ideas among local educators on the themes of inclusive leadership and social responsibility. Such conferences serve as good vehicles for undergraduate research to be reported by education and other majors and their professors, as well as offering an opportunity to learn more about the successes and challenges of implementing reform in the school systems.

Our conversations with teachers familiar with the goals of ELSR reveal the following observations, made by new teachers, regarding the difficulties of implementing those goals in their classrooms and schools:

- Regulatory bodies prescribe curriculum and leave little room for innovation.
- The culture of the school or system discourages innovation.
- Change is associated with a political agenda.

- The 'you have to be careful' norm equates *different* with *problems.*
- There is a fear of job loss, bad reviews, and/or intimidation by other teachers and supervisors.
- Parents and the larger community, who learned with and probably still use a traditional leadership model, may fear change.
- A lack of trust among teachers discourages the sharing of new ideas. There is an intolerance of things that don't work out well the first time.

While the real or anticipated negative reactions come from peers, supervisors, parents and community members, teachers report positive reactions from students (very engaged, noisy, energetic learners) to the use of ELSR curriculums and teaching methods. The teachers also report several conditions that increase the likelihood that an ELSR can be successfully implemented.

- teachers behaving as models of inclusive leadership;
- the whole school as a model of inclusive leadership;
- the overt support of the principal and the superintendent;
- an integrated curriculum that allows leadership and social responsibility themes to cut across almost every subject area;
- team teaching;
- making the values of ELSR prominent as the foundation for the school or district;
- living the value of respect throughout the school.

In brainstorming sessions, primary and secondary teachers offered the following components for an ELSR:

- build in lots of choices for the student;
- emphasize outcomes and accountability for outcomes;
- provide children with opportunities to be both leaders and followers and emphasize the importance of both roles;
- use problem-solving, hands-on, and group learning methods;
- demonstrate that there are not always right and wrong answers but there are right and wrong values;
- practice dealing with ambiguity;
- practice setting individual and group goals;
- explore people's relations to authority and the exercise of authority;

- demonstrate the value of difference;
- develop respect for self and others.

This is a good starting point for the building of ELSR for grades K–12 and has application for college campuses as well.

Four-Year Program for Participatory Leading and Learning

While the aim of an education for leadership and social responsibility is to ready the entire student body to take responsibility for creating inclusive leadership, many institutions may want to build a concentrated program of experiences for some students. The danger of a focused program becoming *the* leadership program of the institution must be guarded against and, because of the risk of elitism, some campuses may choose not to build such programs. While we understand that argument and the inherent dangers, we encourage institutions to rise to the challenge of allowing intensive study programs to exist, without the implicit implication that they are exclusionary. Not all students will desire, nor will their other academic and life commitments allow, immersion in the Four-Year Program for Participatory Leading and Learning (PPLL). Entry into the program should be open to those who can make the commitment of time and energy. In addition, components of the program can be opened to students not enrolled in the entire program. Keeping the group non-elitist can be an interesting leadership challenge for program participants. An Advisory Committee composed primarily of student participants should approve applications, which should include a recommendation from the first-year advisor and evidence of some appreciation of the principles of inclusive leadership, as well as a desire to learn more.

What follows is the outline of a program design that offers in-depth study of leadership and the processes of decision-making and problem-solving over four years. Each institution will decide on the appropriate size for such a program, dependent on funding, personnel, and student interest. This proposal envisions accepting 35–40 students into the program each spring, with an anticipated total enrollment of 125–150 students. On small campuses, the entire student body might feasibly participate in such a program as an adjunct to a liberal arts or professional studies major.

The program attempts to capture and integrate many of the activities to which other students are also exposed in a more random way.

It offers the structure to ensure the maximum exposure to leadership learning opportunities during a four-year undergraduate experience. The model can and should be adapted to students who are part-time, will spend more than four years on campus, or are transfer students.

Sample Outline of Activities — Program in Participatory Leading and Learning:

(* = activities also engaged in by others not necessarily involved in PPLL)

First Year

Focus on the College Community

Fall

- **First-year experience course*: Introduction to the concepts of inclusive leadership, social responsibility, ethnocentrism and the common good, especially as they may be applied to the college community.
- *Membership established with some student organization.

Intersession

- *First-year retreat*: an intensive, two-day leadership retreat with opportunities to engage in simulations, role plays, film analysis and creativity exercises. Review and revision of leadership learning goals.

Spring

- *Meals with leaders*: A series of breakfasts, lunches and dinners with faculty, staff and administrative campus leaders for an exchange of views on what constitutes leadership and how it is developed. The leaders should include people who are doing good work throughout the institution. If possible, meals are held in the homes of the campus leaders.

Sophomore Year

Continued Focus on the College and Introduction to Local Community

Fall

- **Collaborative problem-solving skills* taught in several general education courses aimed at second year students.
- *Meals with leaders* continues: Includes campus and community leaders discussing local problems and leadership challenges. The students begin to assess the extent of inclusive leadership that exists on campus and locally and the obstacles to its fuller manifestation.

Intersession

- *Internship* in local community.

Fall/spring

- **Begin taking departmental courses* on leadership and social responsibility, such as psychology of leadership; cross-cultural dimensions of leadership, leaders in literature; leaders in history; interpersonal communications.
- **Participate in student task force on human relations* or the Center for Conflict Resolution. The task force will present programs on social responsibility and problem-solving and will develop programs to increase interaction and understanding among groups on campus and in the community. The Center for Conflict Resolution will train people in the skills of mediation and conflict resolution and will conduct resolution sessions.
- *Meals with Leaders* continues.
- *Begin service* in the local community either attached to the requirements of a course or as a volunteer. Debrief twice a month with others doing service.

Junior Year

Focus on Domestic Issues within a Global Context

Fall

- *Enter mentoring training program* to prepare for new students entering PPLL.

Fall/spring

- *Meals with leaders* continues: Includes state and local leaders, business leaders and participants in the visiting public servants program.
- *Take* at least *one leadership relevant course.*

Intersession

- *Participate in first-year retreat* and establish mentor relationship with new student.

Fall or spring

- **Participate in leadership practicum* in Washington, DC with Partnerships for Learning (off-campus) with debriefing of the experience for relevance to leadership.

Senior Year

Focus on the Global Community and Life Beyond College

Fall

- *Integrative seminar* on leadership with world issues simulation.

Fall/spring

- *Meals with leaders* continues: Includes alumni who establish mentoring relationships with the seniors to help with career transition, representatives from various career sectors and international leaders.

- *Mentor sophomores* in the program.

Intersession

- *Senior Retreat*: How to translate an education for leadership and social responsibility to employers and to graduate schools. Also how to sustain inclusive leadership in a traditional environment.

Spring

- *Career/graduate school tracking* by adult mentors.

At the end of each semester, all students will attend a one-day, off-campus meeting. Using journals kept throughout each semester, the students will focus on integrating the events of the semester and distilling the group's definition of important principles.

Considerable energy and creativity are necessary to produce and implement programs for an ELSR. As with all curriculum and co-curriculum reform, the validation of the effort is found in the learning and behavior of the students. Although we have separated program design from evaluation, the two processes are closely interwoven. In education, nearly all evaluation — of learner, teacher and program — should be formative, to aid the improvement of desired objectives. Evaluation should make things better by being constantly factored into redesign. We turn in Chapter 8 to some suggestions for evaluation of programs designed to produce an education for leadership and social responsibility.

Research, Assessment and Dissemination

From faculty and staff:

> Even though education depends on feedback, when you evaluate me, I don't like it.

> ELSR goals all sound great but we don't know if they are achievable.

> Certain things, like leadership, you just can't measure.

The fear of assessment is real and the fear can stifle creativity and endanger trust. In an academic environment, assessment should be equated not with the danger of failing but with the positive educational processes of research, growth, and dissemination of information to others. A Center for Leadership and Social Responsibility Research and Dissemination sends the correct message regarding the educational context that makes information collection necessary. Data are essential in order to improve programs, elucidate theory and contribute to the growing body of research on teaching, learning and institutional change. Sharing data and their interpretation with others is an essential component of academic culture.

Outcomes

All good assessment begins with a framework of anticipated educational outcomes that spring from educational philosophy and the values supporting it. During the planning process of ELSR, considerable attention will have been given to the consideration of values, philosophy and outcomes. At the most general and powerful level, the outcomes of an education for leadership and social responsibility will be reflected in the lives of the graduates. However, there is also a need to specify outcomes that are demonstrable before the student graduates.

Most campuses are familiar with outcomes goals as a part of the general education reform movement that has swept American education during the past 15 years (Gaff, 1991; Toombs, Armey and Chen, 1991). An ELSR needs to be built on a strong general education program with which it is fully integrated. The traditional learning goals of general education support the leadership learning goals — which are dependent on a grounding in the perspectives and methodologies of the arts and sciences — and are essential to their successful outcome. Many of the approaches that campuses craft to assess the attainment of leadership learning goals can also be used for the assessment of general education goals: for example, a writing proficiency exam can also test the ability to do systems analysis, to find the common good or do values analysis. In any case, a complete assessment program will contain both overlapping sets of learning goals.

In addition, an ELSR assumes that attention has been paid to the in-depth preparation of students in a major area of study. An ELSR campus will undoubtedly produce more interdisciplinary majors and more cross cutting work at the upper levels. Outcomes for majors will dovetail with both ELSR and general education outcomes to produce an inventory of accomplishments by the end of the program of study which define the graduate as prepared in some depth for a job, graduate work or professional credentialing.

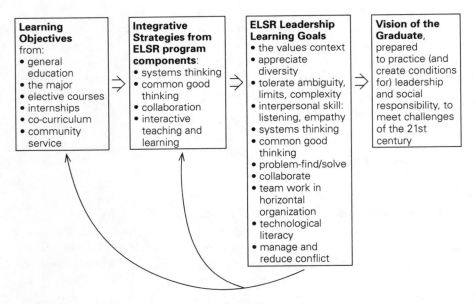

Figure 8.1: Interactive process toward achieving ELSR goals

The Portfolio

The portfolio approach to assessment can work especially well in an ELSR environment (Forrest, 1990). Leadership learning goals, general education goals and goals in the major are largely cumulative. Like most good general education programs, the goals of ELSR are by design infused and reinforced throughout the curriculum and co-curriculum. As goals become diffused, it is more difficult to assign their accomplishment to a particular course or academic department. All ELSR goals and most general education goals are achievable through a variety of means. Still, because it is a straightforward approach, some will be tempted to equate the passing of a particular course with the accomplishment of a learning goal (for example, Introduction to Computers 101 equals accomplishment of the goal of technological literacy). More sophisticated approaches will be required and will be possible with a more coherent, comprehensive educational framework.

The demonstration of leadership learning may be accomplished in a variety of ways: for example, the 'ability to conceptualize a common good' might need the testimony of several faculty and/or student life staff that such an ability was part of a curricular and co-curricular activity successfully engaged in by a particular student. Alternatively, some campuses might feel so strongly about particular leadership learning goals that senior level assessments are conducted within the major via integrative seminars, simulations, interviews etc. All seniors may be required to problem-solve with other seniors outside of their major. These ways of assessing need to be established by students and faculty and approved by faculty to assure some standardization. Lists of ways leadership learning goals can be demonstrated should be published and attached to advising files so both student and advisor can make reference to the individual student's progress semester by semester. The lists can be used for planning purposes as students anticipate their courses and activities for upcoming semesters.

The ideal advising team will be a mentoring team, charged with more than the responsibility for technical advising. The team may be composed of faculty, students and administrators who meet regularly with the student over the course of the years of his or her study. Internship supervisors, alumni or other career relevant people may join the team when appropriate. Participation as peers in such teams may be required by some majors and may be part of the regular work load for most faculty.

Component Outcomes

Four major program components promote ELSR learning goals: curriculum and co-curriculum; teachers as leaders; the campus environment; and community partnerships. To the extent that the following component outcomes are reached, students should reach the leadership learning goals.

Curriculum and Co-curriculum

Exposure to curriculum reforms and co-curriculum programs will educate students to:

- use systems thinking and have resultant tolerance for ambiguity and understanding of limitations and complexity;
- appreciate diversity, individuality and interdependence, and develop the ability to interact productively with people from diverse backgrounds;
- use collaborative problem-solving skills;
- identify a community beyond the self and have a conception of the common good;
- have a sense of personal efficacy and a commitment to the power of groups to affect decisions.

Students will be able to understand and influence:

- complex, interdependent ecological, biological, social, political and economic systems;
- cultural diversities and the created inequalities among groups;
- accelerating technologies;
- networked, decentralized organizations.

When students graduate, they will be ready to:

- create the conditions that foster inclusive leadership;
- assume leadership roles;
- act responsibly on behalf of the common good.

Faculty

As teachers modeling inclusive leadership, faculty will:

- understand their role as inclusive leaders in the classroom;
- increase out of classroom experiences and interactions with students;
- enrich courses with interdisciplinary approaches;
- increase the use of collaborative and interactive learning strategies;
- provide opportunities to explore and integrate systems thinking, conflict resolution, common good thinking, and diversity.

Campus Environment

The offices and people of the campus, in relationship to students and to one another, will:

- reflect values supportive of inclusive leadership;
- promote collegiality, cooperation and awareness of the common goal of student leadership learning;
- increase the representation of diversity within the population;
- create a learner-centered environment in and out of the classroom;
- increase student participation in the business of the college, defining problems and contributing to solutions;
- employ conflict resolution and open communication.

Community Relationships

The college will model inclusive leadership through its relationship with the communities of which it is a part. It will:

- establish partnerships with school districts, community agencies, businesses and non-profits for collaborative efforts to address community concerns;
- provide exposure for community people to the principles and skills of inclusive leadership;
- involve students in learning opportunities within the community.

Formative Program Evaluation

The programs we have suggested in this book are designed to achieve these component outcomes and thereby promote the leadership learning goals. While the effectiveness of the programs and the learning environment will be reflected in the attainment of the learning goals by students, programs need their own on-going, formative evaluation from participants and program administrators. Such evaluation should be expected and welcomed by program administrators.

Training should be provided for project administrators and program supervisors to assure that both qualitative and quantitative data are collected. Prior to implementation of major ELSR programs, baseline data should be collected to provide a portrait of attitudes and activities. On most campuses, data are collected each year for internal purposes and/or as part of participation in state and national reports. Attitudes and behaviors may be indicated as part of information collected for other purposes such as the Cooperative Institutional Research Program (CIRP) study, retention surveys, senior surveys, alumni surveys and catalog course listings.

Operationalizing Key Concepts

An evaluation committee composed of project administrators, faculty project coordinators, students and consultants should operationalize the most important concepts from their ELSR framework. Although no campus can adopt an external set of definitions, we suggest the following, developed by Novella Keith (1992) in response to faculty input and to the authors' work:

Inclusive Leadership

Includes collaborative problem-solving, empowerment of self and others, thinking systemically (holistically), independent thinking (creativity), integrative and interdisciplinary thinking. Inclusive leadership involves the following:

- the ability to learn and work collaboratively.
- knowledge of and ability to use skills of problem-finding and solving and conflict resolution in diverse settings with people of different backgrounds and having different views.
- the ability to encourage broad-based participation and shared authority.
- the ability to engage in self-directed learning and action and to see oneself and others as active, responsible participants.
- knowledge of and ability to trace complex and interconnected patterns related to issues, people, problems and inquiry.

- use of multiple perspectives and creative approaches for expression and understanding.
- sensitivity to limitations, ambiguities and the non-finite nature of knowledge.

Social Responsibility

Includes appreciation of the role of service, ethics, values, and diversity; and a sense of the common good. It shows the following:

- knowledge of and ability to collaborate with those who are socially and culturally different from oneself.
- understanding of how to define and promote the collective well being, and the values of justice and equality.
- understanding and use of ethical analyses to evaluate political and personal actions.

Assessment of Curriculum and Co-curriculum

For the purposes of measuring the effectiveness of programs in reaching their goals, we use the four components outlined above: curriculum and co-curriculum; teachers as leaders; campus environment; and community partnerships. In addition, we add student accomplishment as an area where the impact of the first four can be detected. Chapter 7 outlined several suggestions for curriculum and co-curriculum programs. Though all of them will need assessment, here we provide approaches to assessment for some of the larger campus wide programs.

Individual departmental progress toward infusing the curriculum with materials relevant to leadership and social responsibility. Evaluation may be accomplished through progress reports by departments, revised syllabi, new course outlines approved by curriculum committees, and by outside reviewers.

Table 8.1: *Infusing the curriculum by department*

	leader-ship	common good	systems	realities	ethics	demo-cracy	inter-discip	diversity	tech-nology
Courses reviewed									
Courses revised									
New Courses									

Departments may also be assessed on the degree of participation in project activities. Participation may include work by faculty on committees, use of program content in department courses, involvement of majors in ELSR programs, attempts to connect major to ELSR themes.

Program for Participatory Leading and Learning

Participants in this comprehensive, four-year program offer a captive audience for the use of a panel research design. Data can be collected systematically as students move through the program. Interviews and videotaped problem-solving case studies can provide comparative data over four years. Since these are the students who will be receiving the most intensive dose of ELSR programs, at least in quantitative terms, they should reflect the best outcomes possible and thus become a kind of bench mark against which to gauge the success of the majority of students who are not in the PPLL program. Measures that will indicate that goals are being met include:

- active involvement in the life of the college (count numbers and kinds of activities);
- development of inclusive leadership skills and attitudes (reflected in their activities with others in and out of the classroom; may also be measured by case analyses in first and senior years and by interviews);
- establishment of connections with a network of leaders (count contacts and links made by senior year);
- career plans that include public service or anticipation of bringing inclusive leadership to their workplace and community;
- continuation of involvement in the PPLL program and other college activities beyond graduation.

Program for Mediation and Conflict Resolution

Indicators of the success of this initiative will be both qualitative and quantitative. Numbers of people trained and in attendance at workshops, use of conflict resolution materials in classes, and the involvement of students in opportunities to apply the techniques will be indicators of awareness of these approaches on campus. Those exposed to the process as both mediators and parties to the conflict can assess the utility of the approach. The director of the program should serve both as a referral and clearing house for cases with special care for the keeping of confidential records. Those engaged in mediation will report regularly to the director on the progress of their cases. Records can be analyzed for patterns of conflict, successful and unsuccessful negotiation strategies, parties affected and outcome.

A comparative panel study is another technique which might be used to measure the program's effectiveness. Two panels can be formed, one of people who were trained as mediators, the other of people randomly selected from the campus population. Information gathered from each panel will indicate their involvement with and use of conflict resolution techniques and their assessment of the climate of cooperation on campus. This will permit measurement of activities and impact of the trained mediators and assessment of whether those not trained are affected by the efforts to infuse the campus with the strategies and style of collaborative approaches to conflict resolution.

Case study teams can be assembled by the director to listen to and observe the ongoing mediator reporting sessions. Thus these teams will have the benefit of learning from the analysis of cases as they are unfolding. Students may earn academic credit by using this opportunity to make connections to the academic roots of the conflict resolution process. Papers generated by students in the team will serve as a measure of their ability to integrate the experience into an academic course.

Assessment of Teachers as Leaders

Faculty attendance at and assessment of the various *teachers as leaders workshops* should be obtained each year. The impact of the workshops on course development and revision and on teaching methods can be inferred as well as assessed by faculty. Course syllabi can be reviewed and evaluated. A representative sample of faculty can be interviewed for qualitative illustrations of the impact on their courses and their teaching. Colleague observations and student evaluations will provide feedback on the use of new teaching strategies.

Table 8.2: Sample indicators for annual assessment of faculty development

• Total workshop attendance	• Surveys of attitudes
• New courses developed	• Interviews by consultants
• Courses revised	• Participation in institute/center
• Internships developed	• Participation in PPLL
• Internships supervised	• Participation in community partnerships
• Professional activities	• Visiting public servants
• Classes observed	• Speaker's series

Frequency of *cross-discipline collaboration* to achieve the goals of the project may include course development, team teaching, consultation, interdepartmental sabbaticals and peer observation.

The use of *interactive teaching methods* can be assessed by self reports and by observations. With the consent of faculty, observers may walk through the corridors of classroom buildings at randomly selected times and places and record the observed levels of activity inside the classrooms. Indicants of active student engagement may include the noise level, the physical arrangement of students, the observations of group work in progress and assessment of participation/activity.

Faculty can be *interviewed* to ascertain their understanding of and commitment to the multiple goals of ELSR. Through focused interviews inferences can be drawn about the level of internalization of the philosophy and approaches necessary to sustain the goals of the project. Suggestions for modification and improvement should also be elicited and interpreted as a positive contribution to ELSR.

The *sharing of ideas and experiences with professional colleagues* outside the campus is a good measure of faculty awareness of the significance of ELSR. Faculty can contribute to the development of their professional disciplines by participating in conferences to share their ELSR insights.

Table 8.3: Suggestions for indicators of faculty participation. (Keith, 1991)

ELSR Variable	Faculty Activity
Diversity	• participated in human relations programs; • had discussions with colleagues whose philosophy, etc., are very different from own; • collaborated with colleagues from other areas; • research/reading about women/gender; race, ethnicity; global studies; • course emphasis on women/gender; race, ethnicity; global studies;
Service	• volunteer activities in community; • participated in co-curricular activities for students; curriculum development workshops; other staff development programs; • presentations to community groups; • gave time as volunteer; • worked with students on community project; • signed community service projects/placements;
Ethics and values	• research/read about ethics/values; • research/read about responsible technology; • course emphasis on ethics/values; • course emphasis on responsible technology;
Sense of community: Overall social responsibility/ common good	• research/read about social responsibility/common good; • course emphasis on social responsibility/common good;

All of this can be drawn together in a *faculty teaching portfolio* to be kept over time as a record of course development, observations, teaching modules, reading materials, evaluations of development activities and student evaluations.

Assessment of Campus Environment

Student, staff and faculty attitudes and behaviors should be assessed on awareness of ELSR learning goals, sense of community, sense of personal efficacy, vision of the common good, and awareness of community problems:

- Baseline data through surveys of faculty, staff, administration and students might include opinions about the following:
    - environment for women and minorities;
    - respect for differences;
    - commitment to community service;
    - commitment by members to good of college;
    - a sense of belonging;
    - campus as learner-friendly;
    - relationships among administrators, faculty, students, staff;
    - nature of communication among administrators, faculty, students, staff;
    - use of collaborative decision-making processes;
    - use of teamwork;
    - use of cross functional teams;

Such a survey will illuminate differences in perceptions and may be repeated to assess change in the climate over time.

- Offices should self assess their contributions to leadership learning goals for students and for office members. They may also submit annual plans for increasing their contribution to relevant goals.
- Survey first-year students on items used in Astin's annual CIRP survey, comparing the campus first-year students with the national sample, with preceding classes, and as juniors with themselves in the first year. A measure of program accomplishment would be an increase in the value placed on such items as *serving the community, desire to solve problems,* and interest in *public service careers.* Survey responses can be augmented by cross sectional interviews with representative first-year students, repeated when they are seniors.

- Hire a consultant skilled in the methodology of participant observation to collect data about the cultural climate on campus. This approach will involve observations of ordinary interactions, meetings and communications. These observations as well as interviews with campus members and a content analysis of institutional documents will provide the data for an analysis of campus norms, values and beliefs.

Assessment of Community Partnerships

Community partnership programs are described fully in Chapter 9. Suggestions for assessment of the institution's efforts to be a responsible community member are discussed below.

- As part of the study of campus climate, researchers should obtain data (through surveys, interviews and focus groups) on community perceptions of the college, particularly whether the college is viewed as a responsible and responsive member of the community, providing leadership and partnership.
- Success in obtaining community involvement, including volunteers and resource support to sustain community-college programs, will be one measure of program effectiveness.
- The number of community members involved in programs — institute seminars, mentoring student leaders, community partnership programs — will be an indicator of success in establishing partnerships. The degree to which the college is asked to collaborate in other relevant community projects will also reflect community perceptions.
- An educational consultant can develop outcomes measures for pre-college programs. Pre- and post-testing will establish the effect of summer residencies and longitudinal data will assess the cumulative effect of youth leadership program components. The design should include evaluations by program participants (students and teachers) — which will also influence the shape of the program in the following year — as well as objective indicators of performance abilities. Involvement of college students in these programs and the enhancement of their learning will serve as another measure of program success.
- All conferences, workshops and programs in which community members participate will be informed by their assessment. Follow-ups with local schools and businesses can determine

the impact in the classrooms of community schools and at workplaces.

- Collaborative seminars bring together members of the community with faculty, staff and students to address issues of common concern and produce a useable product for dissemination (case studies, resource directories, teaching modules). As part of the seminars, the participants are asked to evaluate the utility of the experience with regard to objectives, format, content and leadership. Since the participants differ dramatically in their short range concerns — getting through college, running a business, developing a course, continuing education, influencing the legislature — their positive evaluation of the seminar experience will suggest they have identified a common good among them. Use of active learning techniques as part of the seminars can assist in the evaluation. For example, videotaped sessions recording problem-solving exercises will allow both the project participants and the outside evaluators to readily judge the success of the project in improving this skill. Faculty use of the resulting case studies and teaching modules can be measured along with faculty and student assessment of their classroom usefulness.

- The Institute for Inclusive Leadership is a community partnership program described fully in the next chapter. In keeping with the dual purpose of the Institute, evaluators will include academics, practitioners and alumni. Scholars not associated with any of the Institute programs but familiar with the goals of ELSR should be invited to provide external evaluation. In addition, directors and supervisors from the organizations participating in Institute programs can be asked to evaluate the usefulness of their members' participation. After three years of activities, the Institute should have some measures of regional and national recognition and attention received by the campus for its work.

Assessment of Student Accomplishment

The real test of the effectiveness of a revised curriculum and of new teaching–learning methodology is the nature of student accomplishment that results from exposure to it. The following are suggestive of approaches which might be used, in addition to the detailed portfolio, to document the impact of ELSR on student learning.

- Constitute a panel of forty first-year students, representative of the college population. For three years collect data on how they experience, integrate and use the education they are receiving. Most of the data will come from intensive interviews conducted twice a year. Using faculty as interviewers provides a good opportunity for faculty development as well as another important outside the classroom link between students and faculty. Also structure group problem-solving sessions each year, which might be videotaped for longitudinal analysis, to observe growth in the skills of collaboration, intercultural interaction, systems thinking and conflict resolution.
- Other means to assess the ability to work collaboratively in groups include:
  - comparison of videotapes of collaborative problem-solving in sophomore courses, with a problem-solving session in a required interdisciplinary course in the senior year;
  - observations and assessment of active student learning by faculty and by evaluators;
  - replication of comparative studies of cooperative and competitive modes of learning (see Johnson and Johnson, 1994) and their effects on productivity, sense of efficacy and learning.
- We would expect to see an increase in the number of students available for formal leadership positions in campus student organizations as well as an increase in the participation rates in organizations. We expect more community issues to be raised by students — such as the issues of cheating, governance in the residence halls, curriculum needs — and, given the opportunity, more student involvement in the work of departments and the college.
- Count the numbers and kinds of placements available through internships in the major and through voluntary service, and count the numbers of students involved in community service and in study abroad. Correlate public service and multicultural experience with attitude and information changes. Collect evaluations of students by field supervisors and the evaluation of these experiences by students themselves.
- Integrated learning is a highly desirable outcome of ELSR. Data should be collected to verify that opportunities are provided for students to make connections among courses and experiences.

Indicants of opportunities to increase coherence might include: the number of clustered or themed courses, faculty coordination of courses, team teaching, use of interdisciplinary perspectives, use of colleagues outside the department as guest speakers, use of speakers series, Visiting Public Servants Program, films and cultural events as common course experiences, debriefing and group supports for off campus internships, community service and study abroad programs.

- The ability of students to do integrative thinking can also be measured. Faculty may develop an instrument to assess systems thinking abilities which will be administered to a cross section of seniors and first-year students. The first-year students can be retested when they are seniors.

  Components of such an instrument (Keith, 1992) may include the ability to:
    - explain what systems thinking is and illustrate it through an example;
    - analyze the effect of a particular action on a system (a decision at the college, a federal legislation, a personal choice);
    - plan an activity involving others and analyze motivation, planning and decision-making processes;
    - read an article or news report and comment on the system involved, analyze the parts and the effect of change on it.

Another means of assessing integrated learning is the use of common exam questions in coordinated courses (such as first-year clusters and senior year general education courses). The answers to questions of cross disciplinary relevance would serve as a measure of the ability of students to see connection among disciplines and would further serve as a reference for faculty about the bridges that still need to be built.

Hopefully, assessment of learning objectives is itself a learning opportunity for all those involved. It is clearly one of the best marketing tools a college or university or a department can develop. To be able to define what it is you are designed to accomplish and provide some evidence, in the lives of real people, of what has been accomplished is powerful for student recruitment. Most importantly, however, the focus on assessment is a focus on renewal and continuous improvement.

We conclude in the next chapter with a look at the role of community at an ELSR institution. How an institution defines and actualizes community is an important reflection of how it understands the essence of an education for inclusive leadership and social responsibility.

Chapter 9

Building Collaborative Communities

We conclude our consideration of a new approach to education for leadership with a discussion of the meaning of campus community. One of the consistent themes of an ELSR is the role of collaboration in holding systems together and in sparking creative approaches to old problems. We have encouraged collaboration as a powerful learning process for students, as a faculty development process and as a campus governance expectation. Collaboration is relatedness in action, often accomplished in the face of profound differences. Differences enrich collaboration and collaboration is the process through which difference is molded into common purpose. In this way, the process of collaboration functions as an important part of the social glue that holds heterogeneous human systems together.

We have also encouraged the use of systems thinking across the curriculum and co-curriculum and as a teaching tool for understanding classroom dynamics. Systems analysis allows an understanding of the role of collaboration in holding together systems composed of unlike parts and points the way toward an understanding of the common good. To produce students who expect collaborative relationships and know how to organize and use them may be among the most important functions of an education for leadership and social responsibility.

What then is the nature of the campus community that can nurture such students beyond the curriculum and the co-curriculum and beyond the college as an organization? How does the campus define *community*? How does it define and actualize its relationship with its neighbors? What would a collaborative campus community look like?

The Search for Community

The resurgence of a search for community that dominates much popular and academic discourse today is driven by familiar concerns for the survival of democracy and the well-being of individuals. Community, real or perceived, has been related to group cohesion and productivity, social stability and individual mental health. Concern for the demise of community by those who value humane institutions and satisfying social relationships is understandable. Inclusive leadership depends on a sense of community among workers, citizens, students or other members. Inclusive leaders will try to build community through collaborations that highlight common goals and values.

In a mass society where people can remain ignorant of the needs and resources of their neighbors, there is little sense of common interest. In contrast, in a traditional community a consciousness of the similarity among people influences behavior and leads to some conceptualization of a common good: We are all the same and therefore what's good for me is also good for you.

In a more diverse, cosmopolitan society, strong local or subcultural affiliations provide some sense of community. However, they give little comfort to those who recognize the need for a broader identification which can inspire action beyond the local level — beyond the department, neighborhood or club. An increasingly pluralistic world compels us to move beyond some nostalgic goal of re-establishing traditional communities to a more realistic concern for balancing the integrity of pluralistic communities within an inclusive framework. What values and purposes relate the farmer in Iowa and the African American in Newark, New Jersey? What frame of reference inhibits decision-makers from depleting a natural resource or risking war to enhance the national economy? At the heart of the ability to form more encompassing communities is a consciousness of commonality that extends beyond geographic boundaries and is supported by a value for diversity.

Below we sketch three models of college community and argue for a modification of traditional definitions of community so that colleges and universities can be among the first to model *collaborative community*. (See Figure 9.1 at the end of the chapter.)

The Concentric Circle Model

The Carnegie Foundation has recognized the need for a 'more integrative vision of community in higher education', and proposes to explore 'the kind of community every college and university should strive to be'. The 1990 report, *Campus Life: In Search of Community*, defines six principles that, if followed, will unify the campus and provide common purpose. According to the *Campus Life* report, if our institutions could be educationally purposeful, open, just, disciplined, caring and celebrative, we would establish a 'spirit of community'.

The hope expressed in the report is that once established on campus, this sense of community will spread to other sectors and institutions and will ultimately provide a source of renewal for the nation. This concept of reform is based on what we describe as a *concentric circle model*: the college community is at the center, radiating influence, information and example outward. The model is consistent with the widely acknowledged responsibility of institutions of higher education to provide resources to surrounding communities. In this spirit, the college fulfills part of its commitment to public service by providing programming to inform or entertain the surrounding community. The service is generally one-way, from the college to the public. The concentric model is limited and elitist; for many colleges it is also unrealistic.

The model fits best with the characteristics of a small, residential college, a relatively isolated enclave composed of a full-time resident population of traditional-aged students and faculty who live very close if not on the campus. Such colleges provide conditions which resemble those described with nostalgia by social commentators of the early twentieth century as they lamented the loss of community in the face of mass society. We are told that in the 'good old days' people shared similar values and attitudes, there were continuous face-to-face encounters on a near daily basis, and people stayed in one place for a relatively long period of time.

On a college campus, the concentric model is likely to produce a sense of community largely limited to the internal population of the college; even then the emphasis is on faculty and their students, without including staff and non-academic administrators. There is a clear sense of 'we' and consequently of 'they' — sometimes politely referred to as 'town and gown' — and the boundaries of the college are clear both physically and demographically. It is not unusual for these campuses to have walls and gated entrances. In most cases these institutions also have a tradition of and the resources to support self-sufficiency, value consensus and a clear, single-purpose mission.

Unfortunately, the concentric circle campus, which may exist more in memories than in reality, is still used by many as the ideal for the development and sustenance of community on college campuses. 'Residential life provides an excellent setting for consciously learning about community and how it can operate' (Morse, 1989). Even at institutions whose purpose, location and population are quite distinct from a small residential college, this model has become the ideal to be emulated and against which to be measured and found wanting.

Using the residential liberal arts college as the model for community building leads to misplaced blame as to the cause of the lack of community on campuses today. Typically the students and the faculty are faulted. Students are characterized as somehow deficient because they don't stay around on weekends, don't exhibit school spirit and loyalty, don't attend college sponsored events in great numbers, work 20 hours or more per week, and live off campus with people who are not connected with the college. They are defined as less serious and less committed to their educational pursuits than are their counterparts at residential institutions. Likewise a faculty that lives off campus, has family and social obligations away from campus, is part of dual career marriages, and leaves campus offices vacant for up to four months a year, may have its loyalty and sense of community questioned. Rather than capitalizing on the diversity and the cross-cutting community affiliations these complex lives offer, too often we bemoan the lack of campus community and long for opportunities to gather around the fireside and discuss issues of common concern.

Particular Partnerships Model

Many larger, comprehensive institutions move beyond the one-way flow of services implied by the concentric circle model to connect in partnerships with specific sectors of the larger community. The reciprocity between universities and powerful interest groups — the government, the military, and corporate employers of graduates — has a well-established, if sometimes mistrusted, history. These groups have communicated their needs to higher education and have supported academic enterprises with dollars, and higher education has responded with programs, technologies, and research of mutual interest. Concerns are periodically raised, often from within the university, about the ethics of contracted research emanating from institutions of higher education which lose control over the selection of subject matter.

Though the *particular partnerships model* subjects the campus to influences from outside the academy, these relationships are largely functional, involve limited sectors of the university, and do little to build community. The government, the military and industry exist largely as economic partners to higher education. Occasionally, a particular partner is an individual who becomes a 'friend' of the institution by donating large sums of money. The well known Bass case at Yale University illustrated the dilemma for the university when a large gift was made to structure the curriculum in a particular way. Though that money was ultimately returned, other gifts to establish particular programs, renovate facilities or establish endowed professorships have their impact on the character of institutions and the education they offer.

Both the concentric circle and particular partnerships models are inadequate for building the kind of campus community that is needed. With the concentric model, a sense of community exists but membership is limited to campus residents and the external community is often alienated. Colleges and universities with particular partnerships are often fragmented and competitive internally and have little sense of unifying common purpose with surrounding communities.

Collaborative Community Model

Consideration of a new configuration of relationships with a broader representation of community interests is needed if we are to develop collaborative communities that can serve a common good. A connection with the community — from the neighborhood to the globe — is integral to an education that will produce socially responsible leaders and problem solvers for the twenty-first century. If we are to produce graduates who can move beyond personal interests to conceptualize a common good, we must let the community into our educational processes to provide an environment that reflects greater interdependency between the academy and the rest of the world. To accomplish this, it is not sufficient to think in terms of speaking *to* those outside the academic boundaries; we must rather speak *with* and *listen* to voices that have historically been defined as outside.

The reality of the lives of the people in our institutions and the objectives of an education for social responsibility argue for a new conceptualization of campus community that goes beyond the concentric circle or the particular partnerships models. A new model which incorporates collaborative problem-finding and problem-solving linkages with people and interests *beyond* the academy is emerging to provide the basis for community *within* the academy. These learning and working communities will support attempts to educate for broad based, intermittent leadership and social responsibility. They will also challenge assumptions about the academic enterprise.

Traditional definitions of academic purpose, however lofty in the abstract, often pivot around the pursuit of individual interest — getting grades, tenure, a degree, a paycheck, publishing, networking, socializing. A focus on these instrumental goals diminishes the importance of the substance of the interactions that bind us in common purpose — faculty-to-student, faculty-to-faculty, student-to-student, staff-to-student and faculty, administrator to student and faculty, campus-to-community. We rarely ask ourselves what we are doing, or who we are. We rarely have occasion to reflect on the substance and meaning of the processes we are engaged in — learning, educating, problem solving, playing, working. It is those processes that reflect the 'relatedness' described by Parker Palmer (1987) as being at the heart of community in classes, committees, meetings, partnerships, programs. These vehicles must provide the occasion to make conscious our responsibility to one another and to a larger common good.

To the extent that the college broadens its self-definition to include interdependence and social responsibility, we increase the likelihood that we will produce engineers, teachers, managers, librarians and others who will not simply identify themselves as narrow professionals, but will consider acting on behalf of a common good as part of their professional and public responsibility. Since in many higher education institutions a significant portion of the student body is already in the labor force, the potential for impact is immediate.

The same definition of community encourages our college workers — faculty, administrators and staff — to consider the work they do in the context of contributing to common good outcomes. In the classroom both faculty and students are challenged to examine traditional roles as they reshape their relationship and responsibilities. Classroom experiences that promote interaction, employ strategies for collaborative learning, and push the boundaries of a dynamic classroom into the community suggest opportunities for going beyond narrow definitions of teacher and student.

Maximizing human development and the potential for identifying and solving problems requires similar conditions in the classroom, on the campus, or in the community. They include building trust, minimizing inequality of status, encouraging diversity, promoting 'grounded knowing' (Oliver, 1990) and 'creative conflict' (Palmer, 1987). In all three arenas — classroom, campus, community — these conditions can be better achieved to the extent that the essential definition of the campus community includes the integration of people from beyond the official campus structure. In the ideal, we will go beyond conversations with individual, neighboring constituencies and interest groups to discussions and actions that represent the interests of even more remote concerns — from disenfranchised populations somewhere in the city to the ecological welfare of the planet.

Examples of Collaborative Community Building

Programming for collaborative community can be used as a basis for courses, faculty development and co-curriculum experiences. As colleges and universities become open to the possibilities of building collaborative communities — interweaving college and community concerns, responding to people and problems holistically, and linking the classroom with the surrounding world — the prospects for internal cohesion are enhanced as well. The following are examples of initiatives that can be used to open the boundaries of the institution.

• *Community based courses* link classroom and experiential learning and serve community needs. In these credit bearing courses, students spend approximately four hours a week in public service placements in the community and two hours a week in classroom discussions of the academic relevance of the experience. For example, a student might spend the semester reading to a child in an inner city school and studying the sociology of education or the politics of school financing in the classroom. A history course might have students interviewing old people in a nursing home to reconstruct the past with them. Women's Studies faculty might structure a course around volunteer work in a women's shelter with a focus on violence in the family or in a corporate office to illuminate issues relevant to women in the workforce. These courses are a challenge to the traditional model of experiential learning as an individualistic experience, appropriate primarily for its career application. Rather, faculty can creatively use community definitions of problems to guide the choice of course settings in order to illustrate theoretical concepts and promote learning. That these courses may also have career relevance for some students is an additional advantage.

• *Collaborative seminars* provide a vehicle for community people, faculty, administrators and students to work collaboratively on issues of common concern. This approach to public issues analysis and decision-making emphasizes collaborative problem-solving, systems thinking, and the broad perspective of interdisciplinary study. Students might take the seminar for credit, faculty might be compensated with teaching load time or a stipend for facilitating the group, and community members will join for reasons of continuing education, networking and good business.

Seminars or 'think groups' can be established to explore issues relevant to inclusive leadership and social responsibility. Topics of broad interest and immediate application might include: technology and society; creativity and the organization of work; the environment and responsible leadership; women and leadership; pluralism and the common good; children's welfare; and public issues of aging. Each seminar should develop a product, for example, materials to be used in the classroom and/or in the community in order to continue to promote discussion and potentially have some impact on policy.

Community participants contribute the perspectives of a broad constituency — workers from all organizational levels, artists, the government, children, activists, public service agencies — and influence both the choice of seminar topic and the teaching materials that are produced for the college and the community. A few examples of successful collaborations in which we have been involved include: a) a seminar on the environment producing a simulation on solid waste disposal; b) a creativity seminar bringing together performing artists from the faculty and community with business faculty and community business people to discuss constraints on creativity and to develop exercises and management approaches to increase creativity at work. Such a program has been presented to local businesses and professional organizations. In other seminars, c) professors, secondary school teachers, students, and parents developed teaching modules or summer experiences for elementary and high school students, and d) campus and community people collaborated in producing a resource directory for breast cancer survival.

• *Responses to the drop-out problem in public schools.* This is an example of a pervasive and serious problem facing most communities. Institutions of higher education should feel a special responsibility to work with others to improve high school retention rates. It is beneficial for youth, for their families, for the local workforce and community residents, and for the institution of higher education itself. Working with local school teachers, social service workers and local businesses, college faculty and students can develop a variety of programs to enhance the educational success of pre-college students. In some communities a sector of the population that is particularly vulnerable may be selected for attention, such as minority youth, young women, residents of a particular neighborhood. College students can derive academic credit for participation as planners, tutors, observers. A comprehensive approach might include a summer residency on the campus, using campus facilities and participating in campus events as part of the experience. This cornerstone piece can be supplemented by year-round tutoring support, Saturday morning on-campus meetings, and a parent's support group. The ELSR model provides an abundance of organizing principles which might be incorporated into the program or used as themes from year-to-year. Assuming that a student will stay in the program for three or four years, taking on increasing levels of responsibility and leadership, the program can deliver exposure to teamwork, conflict resolution, self esteem, and readiness for leadership and group participation. All this needs to be supplemented by attention to basic skills and peer support for staying in school. Some campuses may be able to offer scholarship support into their college for successful graduates of this program.

Trinity College has provided a recent example (Mercer, 1996) of a more wide-ranging college commitment to help revitalize the city of which they are a part, Hartford, Connecticut. In partnership with four other community institutions — a hospital, children's medical center, mental health facility and public television station — and with a significant combined investment of resources ($175 million), Trinity's goal is to bring back to life a 15 square block area that borders the campus, with an emphasis on the building of several educational sites. Others will surely be watching this initiative as it proceeds, especially for the impact inside as well as outside of the campus.

- *Bringing ELSR to schools.* The principles of an education for inclusive leadership are obviously applicable, in modified forms, at all education levels. Many public and private school systems are discussing such ideas as character education or values education and some publicize leadership or citizenship as a core learning goal. School reform must be organic to the culture of the school, must build on that culture and must be crafted by the participants in the system. An ELSR campus might offer itself as a resource to help facilitate discussion of the ELSR model and participate in ways defined by the school in shaping the application of ELSR to that particular system. The college can also offer itself as an off-site facility for retreats and for summer residencies for students and faculty.

The same requisites necessary for successful implementation of ELSR on a college campus would apply to local school systems. Understanding and commitment from principals and superintendents is essential. What follows are the outlines of a successful program planned and implemented by the Union Springs school district in Union Springs, New York. There the superintendent spearheaded a consideration of inclusive leadership and social responsibility and encouraged its application to the K–12 curriculum. Ideas about site-based management, shared decision-making, quality processes, self-esteem, life long learning, and community involvement in schools had been on the table since former Governor Cuomo's promotion of a state-wide Compact for Learning initiative. This superintendent saw great resonance between an ELSR and many of the themes and goals that were being discussed.

An all-day, district-wide meeting was scheduled (the superintendent cancelled all classes) at which discussion was begun about the framework of an ELSR. The day was spent with faculty from all school levels talking with one another (a rare occurrence) and participating in creativity exercises to clarify their concepts of:

– what twenty-first century realities should we be educating for?
– what is leadership?
– what are leadership learning goals?
– what help do I need to get my students more involved with their education?
– why is it hard to make change in my school?

Following this discussion and an introduction to Teachers as Leaders/Teaching for Leadership, action plans were drawn up for each school in the district. While each school focused on different components of ELSR, they saw themselves — from a student-centered perspective — as one system and communicated via a central steering committee, including parents, teachers and students.

An impressive result of the effort was the construction of a curriculum for a summer retreat for middle school girls and teachers to specifically provide intervention in the recognized derailing of girls from leadership and achievement somewhere around eighth grade. The teachers' own observations echoed the national data (AAUW, 1992) on the pattern of decline in aspirations, self-confidence and self esteem that happens to adolescent girls. Themes included in the summer program were: cooperation, communication, conflict resolution, peer support and empathy, creativity and risk-taking, equality and interdependence, building self and other esteem. These were the same curriculum themes that faculty are now attempting to address for both boys and girls, in all grade levels.

For school systems as for colleges and universities, an ELSR can function as a great opportunity for faculty development. Rather than attending lectures on teaching leadership or character education, the teachers are able to learn by building their own programs in interaction with each other and their students.

• Collaborations with the community such as the one described above can be best accomplished through a visible vehicle, organized by the college to promote ELSR through partnerships. An *Institute for Inclusive Leadership* could be fashioned to accomplish many purposes. It would externalize the mission of the college to educate for leadership and social responsibility by being a welcoming point for community involvement, by facilitating the start of programs to link the community with the college, by providing internship opportunities for students, by supporting relevant research and making findings widely available, by sponsoring conferences, recognition awards and workshops, and, very importantly, by providing a resource for alumnae in their attempts to implement inclusive leadership in their communities, local schools and workplaces. The Institute could offer consulting, planning, programming, networking and researching. As graduates leave the college that has provided them with an education for leadership and social responsibility, they would know that they remain linked to other graduates and to the institution through the Institute. Through contact with graduates and involvement of these alumnae in the programs of the Institute, the College will be able to develop a sense of the effectiveness of the ELSR as it learns from the lives of its graduates.

The Institute can organize and run conferences and workshops that bring educators, business people and community people together to explore the dynamics of inclusive leadership in their particular arenas. The goals and values of inclusive leadership unite groups as seemingly disparate as philosophy professors, small business owners, kindergarten teachers, radio station managers, corporate vice presidents, private school heads, human resource professionals, college administrators, graduate students and professors of French. This is, in fact, a partial list of attendees of a recent conference, organized by the authors, entitled 'New Ways of Learning and Leading'. These people were joined in several days of interaction, learning from each other of attempts to implement inclusive leadership in their workplaces and communities.

Colleges and universities have greatly increased their outreach to local schools during the past decade (Wilbur and Lambert, 1996). School–college partnerships take many forms and result in many creative programs. From an ELSR campus, attempting to establish a collaborative community, all such initiatives must involve community members and students in the conceptual, planning, and implementation stages. An ELSR campus will also attempt to bring the themes of ELSR to the programs as methodologies and subject matter and to involve their own students in the work.

More difficult than a preplanned program for local youth on the campus is the kind of collaboration that seeks to break all status barriers between teachers of little children, high school students and teachers of college students. Collaborations will not work without acknowledgment of interdependence, respect and a sense of equality so often absent from interactions of teachers and college professors today. If we are truly student-centered, collaborations can be developed among teachers who teach in the same subject area or are trying to implement similar methodologies. Getting past old status barriers, these teachers can share teachers as leaders workshop materials as well as ideas for effectively teaching similar concepts and skills at different grade levels. When we bring parents and other 'non-educators' into the conversation, the challenge to learn from one another is even sharper. The purpose of these collaborations is to enrich each part of a student's education to provide more continuity and coherence.

Collaborative Community as a Challenge to the Academy

The challenges posed by integrating the community into the academy are serious and require open discussion. Among the fears and objections that will be raised to a collaborative community approach are the following:

- Linking the campus community into broader community networks outside the boundary of the institution is a potential challenge to the autonomy and authority of the academy itself. Engaging the larger community in the definition of mission, curriculum and co-curriculum may be perceived as an assault on professionalism, accrediting bodies and institutional self definition. There is already considerable resentment about the 'intrusion' of outsiders, especially politicians, raising questions of institutional accountability — including questions about grade inflation, faculty work loads, administrators and faculty compensation — as well as entering or provoking debates about 'political correctness' and the proper content of curriculum. The challenge is to find a balance between the expertise of professional educators and scholars and the needs and perceptions of those outside the academy — not to shut out the latter even when we vehemently disagree.
- The promotion of the vision of an education for inclusive leadership and social responsibility may be perceived as politicized and a challenge to 'value-free,' objective education. The vision of collaborative community and the educational philosophy upon which the vision rests is clearly rooted in democratic, humanistic values. The values are clear. With the value concern in mind, campuses would do well to examine the values and assumptions that undergird their existing curriculums and approaches to teaching, not deny that current programs and approaches are in fact value-based.

- Attempts to increase connections in the curriculum may be a challenge to discrete discipline approaches to understanding. As we increase interdisciplinary approaches, traditional majors may be less attractive to undergraduate students and ultimately less necessary at the undergraduate level. Not only does this potential threaten those trained as specialists in a particular discipline, it also creates the need for different organizational structures to house interdisciplinary approaches. To the extent that faculty have grown up intellectually and socially within the confines of a traditional discipline, the prospect of losing discipline identity will be cause for resistance. The challenge is to honor the depth of knowledge and preparation some of us have, to understand the continuing need and beauty of dedicating one's life to the full understanding of a particular field in order to contribute to its clarification, while building other bases of identity within the academy. The identity of teacher, advisor, colleague and learner can all be enhanced rather than threatened by new approaches to learning and teaching.

- Interactive, experientially-based teaching methods played out in democratic classrooms challenge the lecture format of teaching and the roles of professor as wisdom dispenser, and passive student as information regurgitator. Further, collaborative learning challenges competition as the most effective motivator for learning and tests individualism against the power of teams to promote creativity and growth. Though considerable research has already documented the effectiveness of collaborative learning (Kohn, 1986; Johnson, et al., 1991), fears about the fundamental challenge to the paradigm of individualism and the need for authority will remain.

- The inclusion of service to the community as an important learning component will necessitate appropriate recognition for such service in the reward structure for both faculty and students (Mercer, 1990 and Hirsch, 1996). Service to the community may compete with teaching and research as an important dimension of faculty and student development and as a criterion used for advancement. It is especially important that the stated philosophy and goals of an institution are matched by the reward structure actually used. We have commented before on the need to be clear about the operative definition of scholarship and the ways in which teaching and service may qualify as scholarship, without replacing or demeaning traditional scholarly activities. Given the departure from traditional approaches required by an ELSR, we believe nearly all accomplishments in teaching and service that promote the learning goals of ELSR will be innovative and will contribute to the advancement of understanding.

Although we end this book with a list of anticipated obstacles to building collaborative communities, we are optimistic that the obstacles can be overcome. We have offered a framework for organizing many changes in education that we believe are necessary for successfully and humanely meeting the challenges of the twenty-first century. In doing so we have cared more about raising questions, offering new insights from non-academic sources, discussing processes and providing conceptual links than in constructing a single rigid model. We can imagine that the explorations of others may result in a multiplicity of frameworks that could tap the potential in students for collaboration and inclusive leadership. Although the words may not be used, we believe inclusive leadership and collaborative relationships will be at the heart of any successful reform. Whatever it is called, the energy for change that widens the circles of inclusion is already there. We hope this book will help focus that energy and contribute to the change.

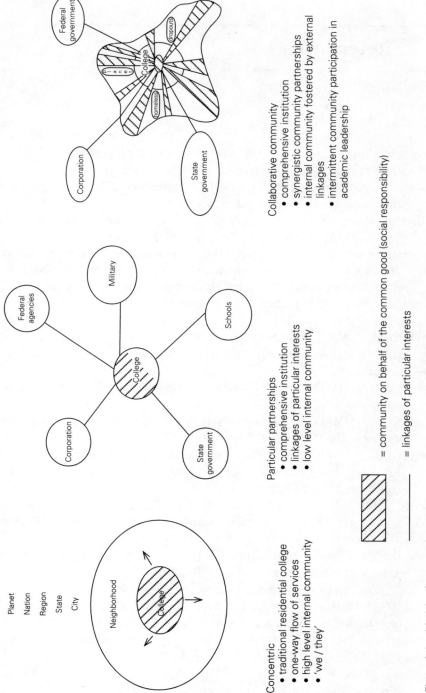

Planet
Nation
Region
State
City

Neighborhood

College

Concentric
• traditional residential college
• one-way flow of services
• high level internal community
• 'we / they'

Federal
agencies

Military

College

Corporation

Schools

State
government

Particular partnerships
• comprehensive institution
• linkages of particular interests
• low level internal community

Federal
government

College

dropout

homeless

Corporation

State
government

Collaborative community
• comprehensive institution
• synergistic community partnerships
• internal community fostered by external
  linkages
• intermittent community participation in
  academic leadership

= community on behalf of the common good (social responsibility)

= linkages of particular interests

Figure 9.1: Models of community

References

ALTBACH, P. and LEWIS, L. (1995) 'Professorial attitudes — An international survey', *Change*, November/December, p. 56.

ARONOWITZ, S. and GIROUX, H. (1991) *Postmodern Education*, Minneapolis, MN, University of Minnesota.

AMERICAN ASSOCIATION OF UNIVERSITY WOMEN (1992) *How Schools Shortchange Girls*, Washington, DC, AAUW Foundation.

ASSESSMENT AT ALVERNO COLLEGE (1985) Milwaukee, Alverno College.

ASTIN, A. (1988) 'The implicit curriculum: What are we really teaching our undergraduates?', *Liberal Education*, January/February, **74**, 1.

ASTIN, A. (1993) *What Matters in College?*, San Francisco, CA, Jossey-Bass.

AUDETTE, R. (1990) 'Meeting the challenge of educational reform: The fourth wave — Deming goes to school', *Small College Creativity*, Winter, pp. 26–42.

AXELROD, R. (1984) *The Evolution of Cooperation*, New York, Basic Books.

BARBER, B.R. (1992) *An Aristocracy of Everyone: The Politics of Education and the Future of America*, New York, Ballantine.

BARR, R.B. and TAGG, J. (1995) 'From teaching to learning — A new paradigm for undergraduate education', *Change*, November/December, pp. 13–25.

BARRY, J. (1996) 'Adrift in Annapolis', *The Washington Post*, March 31.

BEANE, J. (1990) *Affect in the Curriculum: Toward Democracy, Dignity, and Diversity*, New York, Teachers College.

BECKMAN, M. (1990) 'Collaborative learning: Preparation for the workplace and democracy?', *College Teaching*, **38**, 4, pp. 128–33.

BELLAH, R.N., MADSEN, R., SULLIVAN, W.M., SWIDLER, A. and TIPTON, S.M. (1985) *Habits of the Heart: Individualism and Commitment in American Life*, Berkeley, University of California.

BELLAH, R.N., MADSEN, R., SULLIVAN, W.M., SWIDLER, A. and TIPTON, S.M. (1991) *The Good Society*, New York, Knopf.

BENSIMON, E.M. and NEUMANN, A. (1993) *Redesigning Collegiate Leadership*, Baltimore, MD, Johns Hopkins University.

BEYER, L. (1996) (Ed) *Creating Democratic Classrooms*, New York, Teachers College.

BEYER, L. and LISTON, D. (1996) *Curriculum in Conflict*, New York, Teachers College.

BLOCK, P. (1993) *Stewardship*, San Francisco, CA, Berrett-Koehler.

BOYER, E. (1990) *Scholarship Reconsidered*, Princeton, NJ, Carnegie Foundation.

BRICKER, D. (1989) *Classroom Life as Civic Education*, New York, Teachers College.

BRUFFEE, K. (1993) *Collaborative Learning*, Baltimore, MD, Johns Hopkins University.

BRUFFEE, K. (1995) 'Sharing our toys: Cooperative learning versus collaborative learning', *Change*, January/February, pp. 12–18.

BURNS, J.M. (1978) *Leadership*, New York, Harper and Row.

CARNEGIE FOUNDATION FOR THE ADVANCEMENT OF TEACHING (1990) *Campus Life: In Search of Community*, Princeton, NJ, Princeton University.

CHABOTAR, K. (1995) 'Managing participative budgeting in higher education', *Change*, September/October, pp. 21–9.

CHALEFF, I. (1995) *The Courageous Follower*, San Francisco, CA, Berrett-Koehler.

CHAPPELL, T. (1993) *The Soul of a Business: Managing for Profit and the Common Good*, New York, Bantam.

CLARK, K.E. and CLARK, M.B. (1994) *Choosing to Lead*, Charlotte, NC, Leadership Press.

CLARK, M.B. and FREEMAN, F.H. (1990) (Eds) *Leadership Education 1990: A Source Book*, Greensboro, NC, Center for Creative Leadership.

CLARK, M.B., FREEMAN, F.H. and BRITT, S.K. (1987) *Leadership Education '87: A Source Book*, Greensboro, NC, Center for Creative Leadership.

COMER, J. (1980) *School Power*, New York, Free Press.

CONGER, J.A. (1992) *Learning to Lead*, San Francisco, CA, Jossey-Bass.

CONGER, J.A. and KANUNGO, R.N. (1988) *Charismatic Leadership*, San Francisco, CA, Jossey-Bass.

CORNESKY, R., McCOOL, S., BYRNES, L. and WEBER, R. (1991) *Implementing Total Quality Management in Higher Education*, Madison, WI, Magna.

CSIKSZENTMIHALYI, M. (1990) 'The domain of creativity', in RUNCO, M. and ALBERT, R.S. (Eds) *Theories of Creativity*, Newbury Park, CA, Sage., 190–212.

DEMING, W.E. (1986) *Out of the Crisis*, Cambridge, MA, MIT.

DePREE, M. (1989) *Leadership is an Art*, New York, Doubleday.

References

DePree, M. (1992) *Leadership Jazz*, New York, Currency Doubleday.

Donnithorne, L.R. (1993) *The West Point Way of Leadership*, New York, Currency Doubleday.

Drucker, P. (1993) *Post-Capitalist Society*, New York, Harper Business.

Durkheim, E. (1933, 1893) *The Division of Labor in Society*, New York, Macmillan.

Easton, D. and Dennis, J. (1969) *Children in the Political System*, New York, McGraw-Hill.

Edwards, B. (1986) *Drawing on the Artist Within*, New York, Simon and Shuster.

'Fact file: This year's freshmen: A statistical profile', *The Chronicle of Higher Education*, January 12, 1996, p. A34.

Forrest, A. (1990) *Time Will Tell: Portfolio-Assisted Assessment of General Education*, Washington, DC, American Association for Higher Education.

Freeman, F.H. and King, S.N. (1992) (Eds) *Leadership Education 1992–1993: A Source Book*, Greensboro, NC, Center for Creative Leadership.

Friedman, E., Kolmar, W.K., Flint, C.B. and Rothenberg, P. (1996) *Creating an Inclusive College Curriculum*, New York, Teachers College Press.

Gaff, J. (1991) *New Life for the College Curriculum*, San Francisco, CA, Jossey-Bass.

Gardner, H. (1995) *Leading Minds*, New York, Basic Books.

Gardner, H. (1991) *The Unschooled Mind: How Children Think and How Schools Should Teach*, New York, Basic Books.

Gardner, J. (1989) *On Leadership*, New York, Free Press.

Gilligan, C. (1982) *In a Different Voice*, Cambridge, MA, Harvard.

Gilbert, S. (1996) 'Making the most of a slow revolution', *Change*, March/April, pp. 10–23.

Goodlad, J. (1984) *A Place Called School: Prospects for the Future*, New York, McGraw-Hill.

Goodlad, J. (1990) *Teachers for Our Nation's Schools*, San Francisco, CA, Jossey-Bass.

Henry, W. (1994) *In Defense of Elitism*, New York, Doubleday.

Hirsch, D. (1996) 'An Agenda for Involving Faculty in Service', *AAHE Bulletin*, May, pp. 7–9.

Hoffman, M. (1981) 'Development of the motive to help others', in Adelson, J. (Ed) *Handbook of Adolescent Psychology*, New York, Wiley.

Hutchings, P. (1986) 'Some late night thoughts on teaching creativity', *AAHE Bulletin*, December, pp. 9–14.

HUTCHINGS, P., MARCHESE, T. and WRIGHT, B. (1991) *Using Assessment to Strengthen General Education*, Washington, DC, American Association for Higher Education.

JEAVONS, T. (1991) *Learning for the Common Good*, Washington, DC, Association of American Colleges.

JERVIS, K. and MONTAG, C. (1991) (Eds) *Progressive Education for the 1990s*, New York, Teachers College.

JOHNSON, D.W. and JOHNSON, F. (1994) *Joining Together: Group Theory and Group Skills*, Boston, MA, Allyn and Bacon.

JOHNSON, D.W., JOHNSON, R.T. and SMITH, K. (1991) *Cooperative Learning*, ASHE-ERIC Higher Education Report, 4, Washington, DC, George Washington University.

KEITH, N. (1991) 'Report on findings from Monmouth College faculty and administration survey', unpublished.

KEITH, N. (1992) 'Evaluation plan for basic learning goals', unpublished.

KNELLER, G.F. (1965) *The Art and Science of Creativity*, New York, Holt, Rinehart.

KOHLBERG, L. (1978) 'Revisions in the theory and practice of moral development', in DAMON, W. (Ed) *Moral Development: New Directions for Child Development*, 2, San Francisco, CA, Jossey-Bass.

KOHN, A. (1986) *No Contest: The Case against Competition*, Boston, MA, Houghton Mifflin.

KOUZES, J.M. and POSNER, B.Z. (1993) *Credibility*, San Francisco, CA, Jossey-Bass.

KRIESBERG, S. (1992) *Transforming Power: Domination, Empowerment, and Education*, CA, New York, SUNY Press.

LAWLER, E.E. (1992) *The Ultimate Advantage*, San Francisco, CA, Jossey-Bass.

LICKONA, T. (1991) *Educating for Character*, New York, Bantam.

MARCHESE, T. (1995) 'Editorial: Getting smarter about teaching', *Change*, September/October, p. 4.

MERCER, J. (1990) 'Colleges must rethink their concept of service, many say', *Black Issues in Higher Education*, October 11.

MERCER, J. (1996) 'Building hope in a city', *The Chronicle of Higher Education*, March 15, p. A35.

MICHAEL, D. (1973) *On Learning to Plan — and Planning to Learn*, San Francisco, CA, Jossey-Bass.

MILES, R.E. and SNOW, C.C. (1986) 'Organizations: New concepts for new forms', *California Management Review*, **27**, p. 3.

MORRISON, A.M. (1992) *The New Leaders*, San Francisco, CA, Jossey-Bass.

MORSE, S. (1989) *Renewing Civic Capacity*, ASHE-ERIC Higher Education Report, 8, Washington, DC, George Washington University.

References

NANUS, B. (1992) *Visionary Leadership*, San Francisco, CA, Jossey-Bass.

NEMEROWICZ, G. (1979) *Children's Perceptions of Gender and Work Roles*, New York, Praeger.

NEMEROWICZ, G. and ROSI, E. (1990) 'Education for leadership and social responsibility', *Perspectives*, **20**, 2, pp. 21–31.

NEUMANN, A. (1993) 'College planning: A cultural perspective', *Journal For Higher Education Management*, Winter/Spring.

OLIVER, D. (1989) *Education, Modernity, and Fractured Meaning*, Albany, NY, SUNY Press.

OLIVER, D. (1990, Summer) 'Grounded knowing: A postmodern perspective on teaching and learning', *Education Leadership*.

O'TOOLE, J. (1995) *Leading Change*, San Francisco, CA, Jossey-Bass.

PALMER, P. (1987) 'Community, conflict, and ways of knowing', *Change*, September/October.

PASCARELLA, E. and TERENZINI, P. (1991) *How College Affects Students*, San Francisco, CA, Jossey-Bass.

RICHARDS, D. (1995) *Artful Work*, San Francisco, CA, Berrett-Koehler.

ROSEN, R. (1991) *The Healthy Company*, Los Angeles, CA, Tarcher.

ROST, J.C. (1991) *Leadership for the Twenty-First Century*, Westport, CT, Praeger.

RUNCO, M.A. and ALBERT, R.S. (1990) (Eds) *Theories of Creativity*, Newbury Park, CA, Sage.

SARASON, S.B. (1993) *The Case for Change: Rethinking the Preparation of Educators*, San Francisco, CA, Jossey-Bass.

SAYLES, L.R. (1993) *The Working Leader*, New York, Free Press.

SCHANK, R. (1988) *The Creative Attitude*, New York, Macmillan.

SCHRAGE, M. (1990) *Shared Minds: The New Technologies of Collaboration*, New York, Random House.

SENGE, P. (1990) *The Fifth Discipline: The Art and Practice of the Learning Organization*, New York, Doubleday.

SCOTT, M. and ROTHMAN, H. (1994) *Companies with a Conscience*, New York, Citadel.

SEYMOUR, D. (1992) *On Q: Causing Quality in Higher Education*, New York, American Council on Education/Macmillan.

SHOR, I. (1987) *Critical Teaching and Everyday Life*, Chicago, IL, University of Chicago.

SHOR, I. (1992) *Empowering Education*, Chicago, IL, University of Chicago.

SIZER, T. (1992) *Horace's School: Redesigning the American High School*, Boston, MA, Houghton Mifflin.

SLOAN, D. (1996) 'Theoretical foundations of the new leadership: Gilligan, Deming, and Nemerowicz and Rosi', *Journal of Leadership Studies*, **3**, 1, pp. 105–22.

Statistical Abstracts of the US, 1994.

STARRATT, R. (1993) *The Drama of Leadership*, London, Falmer Press.

SULLIVAN, W. (1986) *Reconstructing Public Philosophy*, Berkeley, CA, University of California.

TERRY, R.W. (1993) *Authentic Leadership*, San Francisco, CA, Jossey-Bass.

TOOMBS, W., ARMEY, M. and CHEN, A. (1991) 'General education: An analysis of contemporary practice', *Journal of General Education*, **40**, pp. 102–18.

TOOMBS, W. and TIERNEY, W. (1991) *Meeting the Mandate: Renewing the College and Departmental Curriculum*, ASHE-ERIC Higher Education Report, 6, Washington, DC, George Washington University.

VAILL, P. (1989) *Managing as a Performing Art*, San Francisco, CA, Jossey-Bass.

WEBER, M. (1947, 1924) *The Theory of Social and Economic Organization*, (PARSONS, T. (Ed) HENDERSON, A.M. and PARSONS, T. trans.), New York, Free Press.

WILBUR, F. and LAMBERT, L. (1996) *Linking America's Schools and Colleges*, Washington, DC, American Association for Higher Education and Anker.

WILLS, J. (1995) 'The post post-modern university', *Change*, March/April, p. 59–62.

WOLVERTON, M. (1994) *A New Alliance: Continuous Quality and Classroom Effectiveness*, ASHE-ERIC Higher Education Report, 6, Washington, DC, The George Washington University.

ZEMSKY, R. and MASSY, W. (1995) 'Toward an understanding of our current predicaments', *Change*, November/December 1995, p. 47.

Index

Index